The Secret to Managing Gen Z:

The Handbook

by Janet Granger

Copyright @ Janet Granger, 2024

All Rights Reserved.

ISBN:

9798343346534

No part of this publication may be reproduced, stored in a retrieval system, or transmitted in any form or by any means, electronic, mechanical, photocopy, recording, or otherwise, without prior written permission of the copyright owner. Nor can it be circulated in any form of binding or cover other than that in which it is published and without similar condition including this condition being imposed on subsequent publisher. Any queries related to this publication or author may be sent to janet@janetgranger.com.

Bulk discounts are available to use for corporate training programs. For details, email janet@janetgranger.com.

The Secret to Managing Gen Z:
The Handbook

This book is dedicated to my sons, David and Scott, who've kept me on my toes and helped me stay in touch with younger generations.

Table of Contents

Introduction	1
1 - Let Me Tell You a Story	7
2 - Is There a Problem in Your Workplace NOW?	13
3 - The 10 Deep Dark Secrets of Gen Z	39
4 - What's Different About Interviewing and Hiring Gen Z	49
5 - What's Different About Onboarding and Training Gen Z	61
6 - How to Keep Gen Z Employees	71
7 - Why So Many Millennials are in Leadership Positions	87
8 - A Brief Explanation of the Generation Framework	91
Selected Bibliography	97

The Secret to Managing Gen Z: The Handbook

Introduction

There's a quiet war being waged in the workplace that few people are talking about. It's the war between the generations.

If you think I'm exaggerating, here's what's going on behind the scenes. I've collected some of these comments from **FairyGodBoss.com,** where I recently asked for feedback on what it's like to work with Gen Z and anyone of another generation.

Here are three examples of the comments I received, which were all "upvoted" by other people:

> *1) Make sure you as a manager are prepared to take on rush deadlines because Gen Z won't get it done.*
>
> *2) Make sure if you have something for a Gen Z to do, you give them 3 weeks to get it done.*
>
> *3) Be prepared to have back up available for Gen Z and all the mental health breaks and days off they will need, including the time spent during the day to talk to their therapist.*
>
> *4) Make sure you give them plenty of slack so they can eat, color, do crafts, surf the internet, play their games.*
>
> *5) Don't even bother to tell them there is a dress code because they will totally revolt against it because they want to wear what they want.*

Tell them to grow up, don't be abusive in the workplace, sabotage is never acceptable, high levels of interpersonal aggression will get you fired, criticism is not personal. Gen Z tend to be absolutely horrid to older people and to each other.

1. *Set clear expectations for performance and resulting outcomes. Yes, it's work and you are expected to meet set standards. We can talk about a promotion only after you've contributed above and beyond what's expected.*

2. *It's ok to use sick time as needed but it should be used appropriately.*

3. *Jobs are work and sometimes you won't like it. However, you need to understand how to cope. You will "have to put up with that crap" on occasion.*

The hostility in these comments tells me we have a real problem. Can you feel it in the tone? Or maybe you've got stories of your own bubbling, with frustrations about how you've been treated, how difficult it is to manage others, or to be managed by someone who has no idea what it's like to sit in your chair and live in your life.

If you've nodded yes to any of this, this book is for you.

Bravo for realizing that - while there may be issues between the generations - YOU have the ability to help fix this. I'm going to show you how, step-by-step, from the job descriptions you write to attract and hire younger workers to how you manage them once they are on your team.

How big is this generational issue?

When it comes to Gen Z, Abode has done a survey of hiring managers, and 74% say Gen Z is the most difficult age group to manage in the workplace. (https://www.abodehr.com/blog/what-you-need-to-recruit-and-retain-gen-z)

With the perception among hiring managers that younger employees (Gen Z) are the most difficult, how can organizations continue to operate, grow, and thrive? Especially when Gen Z comprises so much of the workforce, especially for small businesses.

Proportion of Gen Z in the small business workforce

According to a 2023 Paychex report on Gen Z in the workplace, (https://www.paychex.com/sites/default/files/2023-05/gen-z-report-2023.pdf), Gen Z workers surpassed Baby Boomers in terms of small business participation in July 2022. In fact, one in five workers in small business is now a Gen Z.

Here's how the breakdown looks, by industry, across small businesses in the U.S. With national representation at 19%, Gen Z comprises 37% (over one-third) of the workforce in the Leisure and Hospitality industry of small businesses. On the other hand, these younger employees are represented below the national average in Manufacturing and Financial Activities.

Small Business Generation Z Workers by Industry

Industry	Overall	Female	Male
National	19.1%	20.5%	17.7%
Construction	15.5%	12.6%	16.3%
Education and Health Services	17.1%	17.6%	15.3%
Financial Activities	13.7%	13.6%	13.3%
Leisure and Hospitality	37.2%	39.5%	34.9%
Manufacturing	12.8%	14.6%	12.0%
Other Services (except Public Administration)	19.1%	20.8%	17.8%
Professional and Business Services	15.7%	16.4%	15.0%
Trade, Transportation, and Utilities	18.6%	21.8%	16.5%

Whether you work in small business or an international conglomerate, Gen Z is here to stay and this book will prepare you for how they are different from the generations that came before.

Other books have been written about managing Gen Z but, most notably, they were written and before the COVID-19 pandemic. And while COVID didn't change everything - it did change some aspects of the workplace. This book takes those changes into account.

In addition, please note **that this book is NOT a general reference on how to do HR well**: recruit, hire, onboard, train.

There are many books on that topic and I recommend that you continue with the best practices for HR.

This is about the particularities of hiring and retaining Gen Z. It's to be used as an added guide for younger employees, who will comprise 30% of the U.S. workforce by 2030.

In each chapter, we'll review what makes this particular generation different - describing techniques on how you can be more successful working with them. Let's get started.

The Secret to Managing Gen Z: The Handbook

The Secret to Managing Gen Z: The Handbook

Chapter 1 – Let Me Tell You a Story

One of the best ways to help you understand your Gen Z employees is to tell you three stories. These short life stories not only provide insight into their lives and minds but also help you to understand how they think and what makes them tick.

As Simon Sinek says: it's all about empathy. If you get into the mindset of these younger employees, you'll begin to understand why they are acting as they do.

Lacey

Lacey was born 1997. During her childhood, here's what happened in her world:

- **Google** was launched in 1998

- On 9/11 in 2001, the U.S. experienced the worst attack on U.S. soil since the Japanese bombed Pearl Harbor in 1941. 19 hijackers - inspired by Islamist extremism - kill nearly 3,000 people after crashing three passenger-laden commercial aircraft into the World Trade Center towers in lower Manhattan and the Pentagon in Arlington, Virginia. A fourth plane, United Airlines 93, crashes in Somerset County, Pennsylvania, after passengers and crew attempt to regain control of the plane headed Washington D.C.

- In 2002, **the Homeland Security Act** represented the biggest government reorganization of national security efforts since the Department of Defense was created in

1947. It created the Department of Homeland Security, responsible for everything from protecting infrastructure from cyber-attacks to managing **the new U.S. Immigration and Customs Enforcement (ICE) agency.**

- The **U.S. invades Iraq.** In 2003, the United States begins its invasion of Iraq with a rapid bombing "Shock and Awe" campaign to destroy Iraq's alleged weapons of mass destruction; the weapons are never found.

- In 2004, Mark Zuckerberg, a Harvard University student, creates **"The Facebook,"** a local social networking site named after the orientation materials that profiles students and faculty and is given to incoming college freshmen. 16 years later, Facebook is a $843.6 billion digital advertising force so integral to people's lives that it is criticized for helping foreign powers and propagandists influence the U.S. political system.

- In 2007, Apple CEO Steve Jobs introduces the **iPhone,** which becomes the world's most popular branded consumer electronic devices in history.

- In 2008, The Dow Jones Industrial Average dropped of 777 points in one day, after Congress rejects a massive $700 billion bailout of U.S. banks. This led to months of global market turmoil and a U.S. subprime mortgage market crash, creating **a global financial crisis.**

- Also in 2008, **Barack Obama** is sworn in as the first African American president of the United States. Obama inherits **the worst economic crisis since the Great Depression.**

- **Lacey's father lost his job in 2009** as fallout during the multi-year financial recession. At that time, Lacey's mother was an at-home mother, raising three children.

- In 2010, Lacey's father was still unemployed and **the family lost their home**. They moved to an apartment near her grandparent's house in another state. During this upheaval, Lacey was 12 years old. Her family would not be financially stable again for five years.

- Running on a populist agenda, **Donald Trump is elected the 45th president** of the United States and the fifth president in U.S. history (the second since the 2000) to win despite losing the popular vote in 2016.

That same year, Lacey took out the first of what amounted to **$60,000 in loans**, co-signed by her father, to go to college. She is able to get an entry-level job when she graduates and still lives with her parents.

In 2024, Lacey is 27 yrs. old.

Michael

Michael was born 1999, just two years after Lacey. He and his family witnessed the same events - with his experience being two years behind Lacey's.

Luckily, Michael's father, who is an electrician, didn't lose his job and his mother also kept working as a bookkeeper for an insurance company. Michael had an older sister, who looked after him when he was younger and their parents were working. They also attended a daycare program at their local church - before and after school.

Both Michael and his sister were encouraged by their parents to go to college. They believed that a four-year degree would prepare them for better jobs. Living in Florida, the parents had the opportunity to put money into the Bright Futures Scholarship program and encouraged both children to do well in school.

Michael's sister received her scholarship funding with intentions of becoming a nurse. Michael entered school in the fall of 2017. He did well until his junior year (2019-2020) when his school was shut down, due to COVID.

Michael went home and finished the school year online. He thought he'd be going back to campus in the fall but ended up doing most of his senior year remotely. He was lonely and hated the online experience. He missed seeing his friends and having a social life on campus.

His graduation was virtual, by Zoom. It was in 2022, when businesses were just coming back (though in Florida they'd started to open up sooner). Unfortunately, there was a lot more competition for entry-level jobs so Michael wasn't able to get anything in his Communications major.

Michael has been living at home with his parents since 2020. He's taken short-term jobs to get working experience but none have paid well or have a future career path. He owes $14,000 in Student Loans and is not sure how he is going to pay them without full-time work.

Michael turned 25 in 2024.

Nicole

Nicole was born in 2000, a year after Michael. She doesn't remember 9/11 or the U.S. invasion and war in Iraq. Because the internet existed before she was born, she's grown up seeing it used all around her - by her parents and at her school.

The Smartphone was introduced when she was seven years old, so she's been aware of what they are and how to use them since she was in grade school.

During the Great Recession, Nicole's parents frequently fought about their tight financial situation. She watched this for three years - until they got divorced in 2012. She was 12 years old and in middle school, where many of her peers, who had phones themselves, were using Snapchat (introduced in 2011).

Nicole's family couldn't afford to get her a phone but she had friends with phones and they played with the Snapchat messages and stickers. She felt left out, not having a Smartphone, but tried to keep up on the school laptop. She watched in horror one night as one of her friends was bullied on Instagram for an outfit that she wore to the movies.

Nicole's mother encouraged her to go to college, to be financially independent. Nicole went to a community college near home, living with her mother; like Michael, she was forced to do her 2nd year of schooling online during COVID, which then bled into her junior year.

Determined to help her mother with a secure job, Nicole made what she thought was a smart move by majoring in Business. And it paid off: she was able to get an unpaid internship after graduation, which led to another job that was full-time, if she passes her three-month "trial" period.

In 2024, Nicole turned 24 yrs. old.

What do all three of these Gen Z's have in common? They've all been criticized for the following characteristics:

- They question processes
- They want constant feedback
- When they do well, they expect instant reward and advancement
- But they have no "loyalty" to any organization or company
- They work to live, rather than living to work - as their parents seemed to do

Does this sound familiar?

If so, note that we'll circle back to these traits in Chapter 3 to talk about the why behind these characteristics - and how to deal with them.

Chapter 2 – Is There a Problem in Your Workplace NOW?

You're reading this book because you want help. But all the advice and step-by-step guidance won't move the needle if your workplace is set-up to be hostile to Gen Z.

What, you may ask, is a "hostile" environment for Gen Z? Here is a list of some of the characteristics of what this generation considers an environment that should be avoided.

1. Low/non-competitive pay for the title or work being done.

2. Expectations beyond the job description.

3. Ageism – for being young.

4. No career development plan or path for career advancement.

5. Lack of technology to make work efficient.

6. Inflexible or toxic work culture.

7. Lack of diversity among the employees.

8. Inattention to employee mental health.

9. Bad behavior is not punished.

10. An incompetent manager.

If you have any of these in place, change them FIRST because they will hurt all your efforts to recruit, interview, hire, train, and retain new Gen Z.

How do you find out if you have these issues? There are two alternatives - or you can do both:

> A. Survey – send out a survey to your employees – all of them or a well-sampled (statistically valid) selection of them – to find out if there is a problem and - if yes - how prevalent the problem is.

> B. Ask your managers if your organization exhibits any of these traits now, and check Glassdoor (and other similar watchdog sites) to see if employees, or ex-employees, are talking about any of these issues in the organization.

Let's look at each of these characteristics individually, to see why these will put off any Gen Z at your company, or looking at a job at your company.

1. **Low/non-competitive pay for the title or work being done.**

Gen Z is native to the internet and has no issues finding out what the salary ranges are for similar jobs in the industry. How do they do this? Here are just some of the ways to find out who's getting paid what.

- Do a Google Search of competitive pay for the title
- Go to Salary.com
- Zip Recruiter
- Ask on Reddit

- Sharing information internally
- Asking outright of colleagues*

When I speak about hiring and retaining Gen Z talent, I hear a wide range of stories about how they are different from previous generations.

One story that stood out from a CEO was about his giving an employee a "bonus" check. Much to his surprise, the employee took the check - which he received in person - and walked around the office floor, showing it to his colleagues.

"I just got this bonus check! Did any of you also get this?" he asked.

The CEO was floored, as were the other CEO's in the room when he shared this story. "He won't be seeing one of those again," was his response to this behavior. And others nodded their heads in agreement.

I provide this as an example of the lengths to which employees will go to provide "transparency" to one another. Their feeling is that the more everyone knows, the better off they all are; knowledge is power.

While this may not be the feeling or the response that's given by senior management, it's something to keep in mind when thinking about financial compensation. This generation has seen so much bad behavior, when it comes to paying women and minorities less than others, that they will share amongst themselves in order to keep the pay equitable.

This is where their passion for DEI (Diversity, Equity, and Inclusion) goes well beyond what's visible to what's not visible, when it comes to pay equity.

On a final note, there are ways to look up how pay equity is trending on social media. For example, on Instagram, Oprah

Winfrey tells the story of being paid half of what her colleague was making. When she asked about it, in 1980, she was told that he "needed" the money more: he had a house, he had to send his children to college. When she said they were doing the same job, she was told no, they were not. (Link: https://www.instagram.com/p/BmLa25onwx0/)

2. Expectations beyond the job description.

One of the best ways to see what Gen Z employees are complaining about to one another is to look at Instagram accounts.

For example, there's an account (and a podcast) called "Not in the Job Description" (Link: https://www.instagram.com/not_in_the_job_description/) On Spotify here: https://open.spotify.com/show/6RC9GbJeZVZp7UTP8PjZjD - with episodes going back to July 2022.

While not everything can be put into a job description, it's critical to put the important items, especially if they are part of the work culture. For example, if employees are expected to answer emails and texts over the weekend or after work hours, these can be seen as "beyond the job description."

Many older workers will argue that "that's how things were done" back in their day. And while that is true for many of us (myself included), Gen Z has seen how an employee going "above the beyond" the job description doesn't serve them (or their families) well.

Here are just some of the examples they cite, which they lived themselves or saw in their parents:

- Missing their children's sports practices or games because they are working after hours or on weekends.

- Not being able to go to family events (weddings, birthdays, etc.) because they were called in to work, or working late.
- Losing time off because they took personal or vacation time to go to medical appointments.

And after losing out on their personal lives, these parents were let go during the Great Recession, or were forced to "retire early" as they approached the age of 60.

After seeing how "going beyond the job description" did not work out for their parents and friends, Gen Z is determined not to be taken advantage of by their employer. If you expect more than what's currently in the job descriptions you're sharing, it's a good time to rethink how these jobs are defined.

3. Ageism – for being young

Do you remember when you graduated from college, or graduate school, and arrived at your first job? I do. I remember the feeling of being ready to take on the world. I came in for my first day and was ready for action. I'd been writing papers about how to solve major questions in the world, or in my field. And I was ready to take my ideas skyward.

I walked into my first job at a major consulting firm after I got my MBA, thinking I would be part of a team that was asked to tackle the most pressing issues for major companies. What did I get to do? Make PowerPoint presentations based on what the team decided (mostly the senior partner).

I wasn't that great at them either; there were others who could make the fanciest slides, with animation, great design that really grabbed your attention. It was demoralizing to think that I'd spent a fortune on an MBA only to become a PowerPoint designer.

Did you have any kind of "first job" disappointment like this?

If you did, that gives you some insight into the disappointment that younger employees feel now. They, too, want to tackle critical problems and issues in the world. Instead, they are relegated to doing the least important tasks. They're in the lowest position on the team, often because that's what leadership remembers happened to them.

This is ageism – treating them as low value members of the team simply because they are young and inexperienced. Don't get me wrong – I'm not saying they deserve leadership positions yet. I'm simply pointing out that they, too, can have valuable insights for the team and shouldn't be silenced or ignored, just because of their age.

Age-diversity on a team and in an organization helps broaden the understanding and vision of the team. Like other types of diversity, age diversity makes teams stronger and better.

I cited one of my favorite examples of this in my previous book, *Ok Boomer! Revelations of a Baby Boomer Working with Millennials*. It shows how having a diverse group of people involved in a project is not only helpful, it can avoid bad mistakes.

Take a look at the image that follows. It's the entryway for a new church building, with three banners representing the flagship principles: Worship, Teaching, and Friendship. But there's a fundamental problem with the display of the banners. Do you see it?

Each banner has the first letter at the top: W T F. To younger people (Millennials and Gen Z), the acronym WTF in texting means "what the f**k?"

If the person or group that came up with these banners had included younger members of the organization, they would probably have avoided this mistake. To me, this is a great representation of the hazards of not including a diverse group of people in any event or project planning.

You don't know what you don't know. Inclusion of different groups, including both younger and older team members, gives you a better chance of not making a mistake because you didn't know.

4. **No career development plan or path for career advancement**

There are as many different types of workers as there are workers. Having said that, it's easiest to simplify the various types of employees you might have into three categories:

- Those who have ambition
- Those who want to be comfortable and feel their job is a constant in their lives
- Those who don't have ambition and want to "just work" and then leave

This section is for those younger hires who have ambition and want a career, not for the second two categories.

For them, they're thinking about this job and the next job and the next. Unlike their Millennial counterparts, they do not want to have to look for a new position every 18 months.

Gen Z with ambition, who want a successful career, typically prefer to find an organization that resonates with them and their goals and their values, and stay there. For them, the question is: where can I go from here?

McKinsey & Company did a survey to workers in the U.S., asking for the reasons they would stay at an organization or why they would leave. The results for Gen Z are a great indicator of how important career development is to this generation.

The first graph (on the next page) is the answer to the question: "why I left my previous job." The #1 reason was "lack of career development and advancement potential." Please also note that the #2 reason, not far behind, was "lack of support for employee health and well-being."

We'll be discussing that later.

The Secret to Managing Gen Z: The Handbook

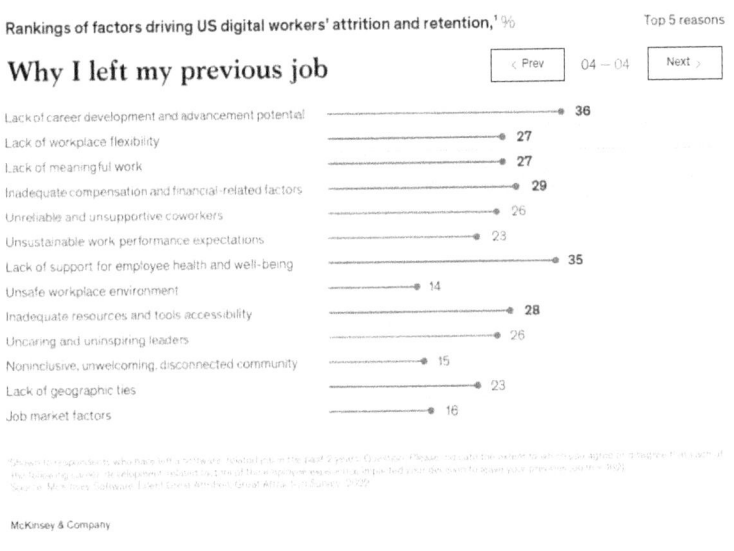

The next graph outlines the reasons "why I accepted a new job." Once again, "career development and advancement opportunities" is the leading reason.

And notice, in this case, it's well above the secondary reason, which is "compensation and financial-related factors." While Millennials may be swayed by a higher salary alone, 52% of Gen Z prizes opportunity first.

At most key decision points, digital workers place as much if not more importance on career development and advancement potential as they do on compensation.

Rankings of factors driving US digital workers' attrition and retention,[1] % Top 5 reasons

Why I accepted a new job

Career development and advancement potential	52
Workplace flexibility	35
Meaningful work	37
Compensation and financial-related factors	45
Reliable and supportive coworkers	17
Sustainable work performance expectations	34
Support for employee health and well-being	16
Safe workplace environment	24
Adequate resources and tools accessibility	23
Caring and inspiring leaders	27
Inclusive, welcoming, connected community	20
Geographic ties	20
Job market factors	15

McKinsey & Company

Deloitte also did a study of Gen Z, to understand what motivates them. Here's what they found: a full 51% of respondents are motivated by opportunities for growth.

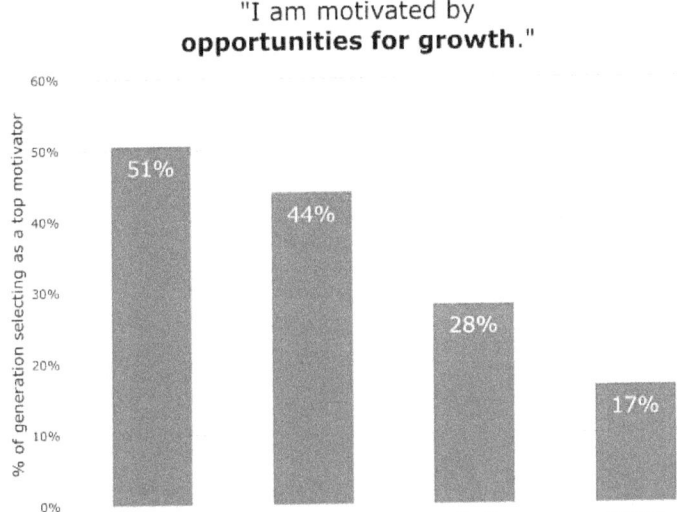

"I am motivated by **opportunities for growth**."

These are the candidates you want to hire because they're going to take their position seriously and care about their work. They are the ones who will stay late to finish an important project (assuming you've told them this happens from time to time). They're the ones who will care about their work and give you their best effort.

If these are the candidates you're looking for, I suggest you think about what a career path might look like for them. Or, if you have examples in your organization of what other career paths have looked like, write up some examples of possible career paths. These can be used digitally (on your website) or shared with potential candidates.

5. **Lack of technology to make work efficient.**

Gen Z has always had an internet, since they were born after 1996. And the older ones (in their mid-20s as of this writing) have had experience with smartphones since 2007, when the first iPhone was released. Many of them had smartphones as teenagers.

Technology that was created to make life easier has grown geometrically in the past 25 years. Here's just a small list of breakthrough technological advances that consumers have seen and many have enjoyed:

- Google
- Google Maps
- Facebook
- YouTube
- Bluetooth
- EV's
- 3D printing
- Wi-fi
- The Internet of Things (IoT)
- Voice Assistants (Alexa, etc.)
- Bitcoin
- Blockchain
- Music streaming
- Facial recognition
- Artificial Intelligence (AI)

Looking at this list, think about what you did before these technologies existed. For example, how did you listen to music? Do you own albums or CD's? How do you listen to music now? As consumers, our habits have changed dramatically over time, as new technologies have been invented and quickly become mainstream.

Thinking about these changes, it makes sense that younger employees are hooked on tech. For many, it's been around as long as they can remember. It also makes life easier.

Consider the software available for communications at work. Slack was invented back in 2013 and has changed the way teams communicate, both within organizations and with outsiders. It's similar to texting in that it's immediate, rather than dependent on another platform (such as email).

Gen Z has been used to texting since they were teens, and using software such as Slack or Google Workspace. They expect these types of software technologies in their workplace, as well.

Do you have an up-to-date project management system? Or customer relationship management platform? If not, you're behind the times, from an organizational perspective. And your lack of technology will hurt you when it comes to retaining your Gen Z talent. They don't want to have to resort to processes that waste time; they expect to be able to use the latest-and-greatest in order to work efficiently.

One great way to take advantage of Gen Z tech savvy, if your organization is behind the times, is to create a task force of younger employee talent to help you figure out the best software. Asking them to be part of the solution, when it comes to technology, is the best way to use their gifts and to engage them in important projects.

6. **Inflexible or toxic work culture.**

The company Abode did research into the Gen Z 'work-trends' and shared the following in their report, with regard to what flexibility means to this generation. Please note that the biggest type of flexibility they desire (36.51%) is for their schedule, meaning the ability to choose the days they work. The popularity of this response indicates that there are many retail and hourly employees who responded to the question, who may find themselves working weekends and holidays.

While it would be wonderful to be able to accommodate everyone when it comes to the days they prefer to work, most retail and hospitality workers who are young will probably have the least tenure and will - therefore - be assigned to the least desirable days.

The next most important area for flexibility is in hours, which may provide more leeway for employers. But again, this depends on the industry and the work involved.

▼ Q6: What type of flexibility in the workplace is most important to you?
- Location flexibility: the ability to choose where I work from - 24.60%
- Hours flexibility: the ability to choose the hours I work - 32.54%
- Schedule flexibility: the ability to choose the days I work - 36.51%
- None of these are important to me - 5.56%
- Other - 0.79%

When focusing in on "work-life balance" in 2024 - a loose idea of 'boundaries' between working hours and leisure time is not enough. Gen Z wants the autonomy and power to dictate these boundaries regardless of if their work contract, full-time, part-time, or hourly. Autonomy is the key to making Gen Zers feel valued today.

The idea of a 'toxic culture' is a difficult topic for many leaders to tackle because there isn't one definition of toxic culture. It can be many things. But solving for a toxic culture may be an easier task than changing work hours, especially in the retail and hospitality industries.

How do you know if you have a toxic culture? Some of the telltale signs are high turnover rates and low morale. While it's hard to change a culture, it will be better for everyone – all generations - in the workplace if a toxic culture is changed.

Here are just a few examples of what makes up a toxic culture.

    A. *Lack of trust*

In a toxic work environment, or working for a toxic manager, there's no trust between individuals. If managers don't trust their teams and senior leaders don't trust their managers, it leads to a focus on 'looking good' rather than performing well. It can also lead to micro-management by managers, which is demotivating to employees.

B. *Blurring of work boundaries*

If employees feel they need to be working all the time, including nights and weekends, it's a toxic work environment. Everyone deserves a life outside of work. This includes a culture where employees feel they can take their allotted time off and go on vacations, without having to answer emails or messages.

C. *No repercussions for harassment or bullying*

A workplace that doesn't punish those who harass or bully others is considered toxic. Examples of harassing or bullying behavior include offensive jokes, insults, intimidating language or behavior, and physical threats. Check out this article about bullying being called out by Gen Z: https://www.hr-brew.com/stories/2024/04/30/gen-z-employees-are-calling-out-workplace-bullies-what-this-could-mean-for-hr

D. *Mistakes are not allowed*

While no one wants to make an honest mistake, they do happen and everyone makes them at one time or another. If there's a lot of blame going around, employees will be paralyzed by fear, rather than motivated to succeed.

To go one step further, it's important to try new things, from software to processes, as a business grows and changes. What may look like a great idea one day may look like a mistake a year later. It's important that the organization allows for mistakes to be made and doesn't punish individuals (or teams) for trying something new.

E. *Gaslighting by managers or colleagues*

Gaslighting means making people question their own perceptions. Examples include excluding a person from meetings directly related to their job, and a manager who belittles direct reports for their emotions or requests. This might include an employee asking for time off for a family emergency, for example, and their manager not believing them, or denying the request.

F. *Excessive stress*

There can be many reasons for employees feeling stressed, some of which can't be changed because they are endemic to the industry. For example, seasonality can cause additional stress at tax time for accountants, or year-end stress for sales and sales support as they try to close out the year.

Uncertainty in the economy can cause stress too, such as rising interest rates in the real estate industry.

Excessive stress, year-round, is something else. It can be caused by employee burnout, because the organization doesn't have enough staff to share the work. It can be caused by inept managers, who don't know how to cope with peoples' problems. It can also be caused by the other elements listed here: lack of trust, no work boundaries, gaslighting, etc., which - inevitably - lead to employee stress and high turnover rates.

If your organization exhibits any of these characteristics, it's time to address the culture. Hiring new Gen Z talent won't make a difference if you haven't fixed the toxic culture first. It's like pouring water into a bucket with a hole in the bottom: the water will just keep running out as fast as you can pour it in.

7. **Lack of diversity among the employees.**

Why is diversity important? As mentioned above, a lack of age diversity can lead to some embarrassing situations (Worship/Teaching/Friends). Data has shown that true diversity across all ages, genders, and social demographics actually creates better results. Here are just a couple of examples.

McKinsey & Company

"McKinsey & Company conducted a comprehensive study on the impact of diversity in the workplace. Analysis of 2019 showed that companies in the top quartile for **gender diversity** within executive teams were 25 percent more likely than companies in the fourth quartile to have above-average profitability - up from 21 percent in 2017 and 15 percent in 2014.

"This suggests that diverse teams are better equipped to understand and cater to global markets, leading to increased revenue and market share.

"In addition, the greater the representation of gender diversity, the higher the likelihood of outperformance. For instance, companies where more than 30 percent of the executives are women were more likely to outperform companies where this percentage ranged from only 10 to 30. The most gender-diverse companies see a substantial differential likelihood of outperformance—48 percent—over the least gender-diverse companies.

"The business case for **ethnic and cultural diversity** is also strong: in 2019, companies in the top quartile bested those in the fourth quartile by 36 percent in profitability. Notably, the likelihood of outperformance continues to be higher for diversity in ethnicity than in gender.

"In addition to profitability, there are five key domains in which inclusion and diversity can significantly affect an organization's overall performance:

1. *Winning talent:* Organizations that monitor the demographic profile of their workforces are better able to retain top performers while making sure that diverse talent isn't lost.
2. *Improving the quality of decision making:* Diversity brings multiple perspectives to the table during times when enhanced problem-solving skills and vision are needed.
3. *Increasing customer insight and innovation:* Diverse teams are typically more innovative and better at anticipating shifts.
4. *Driving employee motivation and satisfaction:* Research in Latin America showed that companies that are committed to diversity are 75 percent more likely to report a pro-teamwork culture.
5. *Improving a company's global image and license to operate:* Companies that can maintain or increase their focus on inclusion and diversity during crises are poised to avoid consequences such as struggling to attract talent or losing customers and government support.

Harvard Business Review

In 2016, the Harvard Business Review published this:

"Diverse teams are more likely to constantly re-examine facts and remain objective. They may also encourage greater scrutiny of each member's actions, keeping their joint cognitive resources sharp and vigilant. By breaking up workplace homogeneity, you can allow your employees to become more aware of their own potential biases — entrenched ways of thinking that can otherwise blind them to key information and even lead them to make errors in decision-making processes."

There are other examples, and all point to the fact that diversity of thought in a group is better because it ferrets out unconscious biases of all kinds, and forces everyone to focus on goals and data.

Gen Z is not only aware of this data, they typically feel most comfortable in a more diverse environment, since that has been their experience. If the goal is to retain more Gen Z employees, one of the first places for leadership to examine is the current diversity of the workforce. It's no longer enough to talk about diversity and celebrate Black History month and Women's History month. Gen Z expects *true* diversity among employees.

8. Inattention to employee mental health.

Gen Z is the first generation in the U.S. to be open about discussing their mental health issues. And many of them have issues. (https://www.axios.com/2024/02/17/gen-z-depression-anxiety-future-workforce)

Due to their familiarity with technology, Gen Z socializes online - instead of in person - far more than previous generations. That means that they don't receive the brain chemical "boost" that is released when we're with other people in real life.

The pandemic made this even worse for this younger generation, who were still in school: college, high school, or grade school.

A study by the Walton Family Foundation on the Voices of Gen Z was conducted in November, 2023. It uncovers some startling data about the prevalence of anxiety and depression in this generation.

When asked to answer on a percentage basis how often they "feel anxious," the number of Gen Z who claimed they Always or Often feel this way was 47%. This was highest among those who self-define as lesbian, gay, bisexual, or other orientation (74%) and those aged 21 – 23 (59%).

When asked to answer on a percentage basis how often they "feel depressed," the number of Gen Z who claimed they Always or Often feel this way was 22%. Again, this was highest for those who self-defined as lesbian, gay, bisexual, or other orientation (50%) and those aged 21 – 26 (31%).

This is illustrated in the following bar chart:

The Secret to Managing Gen Z: The Handbook

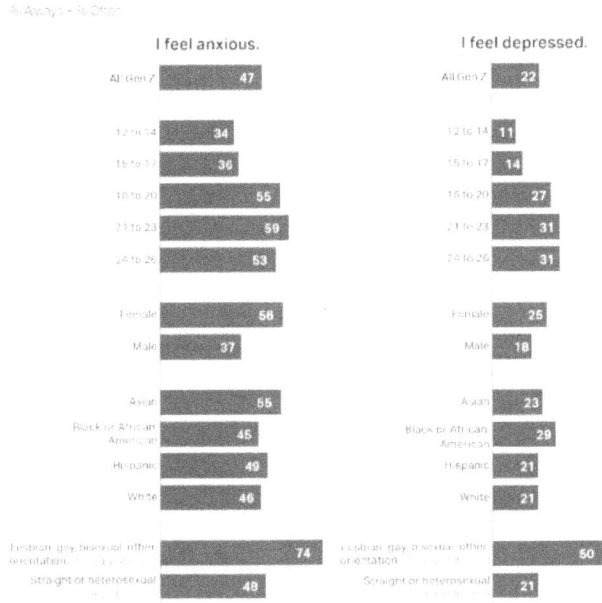

Nearly Half of Gen Zers Are Often Anxious; About One-Quarter Are Often Depressed

Here's more infographic information about Gen Z's state of mental health. This comes from a study done of 1,000 Gen Z respondents age 18 – 24. (https://www.harmonyhit.com/state-of-gen-z-mental-health/)

Statistics to note about this age group:

- 25% were diagnosed with a mental health condition during the pandemic
    - 68% feel the pandemic negatively affected their mental health

- 57% are currently taking medication for their mental health

- o "Nine out of ten Gen Z with diagnosed mental health conditions struggle with anxiety, and nearly eight out of ten (78%) are battling depression"
- Gen Z's biggest mental health issue is anxiety
- 15% of respondents have talked to their boss about their mental health
- 62% have taken a mental health day off from school or work

Gen Z State of Mental Health

42% have a diagnosed mental health condition

1 in 4 were diagnosed with a mental health condition during the pandemic

68% feel the pandemic has negatively affected their mental health

57% are currently taking medication for their mental health condition

Gen Z pays $44 on average every month for medication

62% have taken a mental health day off school or work

Gen Z has taken an average **3 mental health days** in 2022

15% have talked to their boss about their mental health

91% of bosses were supportive

9% of bosses were unsupportive

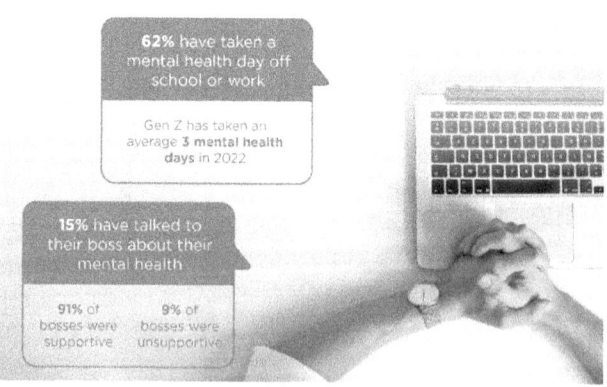

All of this data illustrates that Gen Z has mental health issues that they want to discuss and have the ability to work on. If your organization doesn't acknowledge this issue or is not supportive of employee mental health, it will be harder to retain these employees.

9. Conflict and bad behavior go unpunished.

One of the best ways to lose good people is to let bad behavior go unchecked. This includes the bullying and gaslighting mentioned earlier, as well as other unwanted behavior that makes employees uncomfortable.

Here are just a few examples of bad behavior that should have repercussions in the workplace.

- Unethical or illegal behavior
- Racism
- Sexual harassment
- Bullying or intimidation
- Gaslighting

How big is this issue? Here's some data from a study done by HRAccuity. They surveyed roughly 2,000 U.S. employees across various industries, organization sizes and demographics. They tabulated this information for their 2023 Workplace Harassment & Misconduct Insights study.

- Over half (52%) of employees have experienced or witnessed inappropriate, unethical or illegal behaviors at work.

- The most prevalent of these behaviors were bullying (51%), sexual harassment (40%) and racism (30%).

- In 2023, only 58% of employees reported the poor behaviors they experienced or witnessed.

  - This is down 6% from 2019 – and reveals a growing blind spot of unreported incidents for organizations.
  - There were many reasons why employees didn't report workplace issues, the largest of which was fear of retaliation (46%).
  - One in four (25%) didn't report the behavior because it was it involved a person "more senior" at the organization than the employee.

- 57% of employees cited harassment or misconduct as the reason they left or a factor in their decision.

  - 30% of employees who experienced or witnessed inappropriate, unethical or illegal behaviors left the organization following the incident.

The bottom line is this: allowing bad behavior to exist in an organization leads to employee turnover. One of the best ways to make sure your organization is prepared to retain Gen Z employees is to ensure there's a strong culture of not tolerating this type of behavior. This includes clear language about behavior that will not be tolerated, and a smooth process to deal with this type of behavior.

10. An incompetent manager.

One of the biggest retention issues for Gen Z, as well as other younger employees, is reporting to an inept manager. In addition to the bad behavior we just reviewed, here are the statistics on employees who leave because of their manager.

According to research by DDI World, the Frontline Leader Project in 2019, "**57 percent** of people have left a job specifically because of their manager. Furthermore, 14 percent of people have had to leave multiple jobs because of management."

What was it about managers that made people quit? The list, in descending order is:

- Their manager did not show respect for their work
- Their manager was unprofessional or didn't listen to their concerns
- Their manager lacked empathy

Showing empathy and respect is a skill that can be learned, if an organization takes the time and makes the effort to train first-line managers. However, according to DDI, **the biggest issue with frontline managers is their lack of training.**

Examining the data from their survey data (9,700+ frontline leaders), it's clear that almost half want more coaching (49%) from their manager than they've received, and 57% want more external coaching.

(Source: DDI Frontline Leader Project)

If there is an opportunity to fix your organization before you bring in more younger employees, it appears that training frontline managers in how to manage effectively is a great way to start.

Looking back on these reasons that employees leave, it makes sense to address these issues in your organization, if they exist. (If you're not sure, there is a quick employee survey that can be done to find out!)

While you're discovering whether or not these issues exist in your organization, and established processes to address them, let's take a look at the deep, dark secrets about Gen Z that you should know.

Chapter 3 – The 10 Deep Dark Secrets of Gen Z

In case you're the type of person who skips the rest and cuts to the good part: this is your chapter. It explains why you find Gen Z so difficult to understand.

(Note: it would be really helpful if you read Chapter 1 first, if you haven't already. It's short and provides some perspective on a few individual people in Gen Z. Go read it and come back; place a bookmark here!)

There are good books you can read about the upbringing of Gen Z, with theories on how they got to be the way they are - as a generation. They're in my Selected Bibliography at the end of this book. I've summarized much of what they have to say to give you the salient points: what you need to know in order to attract them as candidates, hire them, and manage them as employees.

Here are the **10 deep dark secrets**, which I'll expand upon in this chapter (this is the TLDR list):

1. They are dependent on technology.
2. They are not used to feeling uncomfortable or ill-at-ease - and avoid it at all costs.
3. They avoid conflicts - again, at all costs.
4. They need constant feedback.
5. They are not resilient.
6. They are risk averse.
7. They have difficulty thinking for themselves and often lack critical thinking skills.
8. But they also question processes.
9. They don't trust authority and have no brand or company "loyalty."

10. They insist in "personal boundaries."

Let's dive into these in more detail, and talk about how to manage Gen Z employees who have these characteristics.

1. They are dependent on technology.

Hannah Grady Williams, a Gen Z herself, wrote a book about how to "unlock" Gen Z. She has some interesting comments about her generation's technology expectations, writing that "the technological savvy of a company is nearly imperative to our successful functioning." (Chapter 5, p. 69).
https://www.amazon.com/Leaders-Guide-Unlocking-Gen-Strategies/dp/1737616521

This dependency on technology is "not because we love technology but because it's what we're used to and we don't know how to function without it in many ways." This dependency cuts both ways, as it also explains how Gen Z can be awkward with people. We've all seen groups of Gen Z out together, sitting next to one another, all glued to their phone screens, rather than speaking to one another.

This dependence on their phones is both a gift and an issue; they don't know what to do without their phones, in many cases. And that is one of their deep dark secrets: they're experts at knowing how to do things quickly and easily using software - and hardware - but this expertise comes at a cost.

One of the best ways to utilize this gift is to put Gen Z in charge of exploring better uses of tech to solve problems in the workplace or in workflow processes. But be careful not to fall too far behind in your use of tech, because a Gen Z won't want to work in an office that makes them do things manually, the difficult and hard way, when there are technologies to make the work easier and faster.

2. **They are not used to feeling uncomfortable or ill-at-ease and avoid it at all costs.**

If you've not watched Simon Sinek videos about Gen Z on YouTube, I highly recommend that you check them out. He talks a lot about having empathy, to manage this age group, and is candid about having difficulties with his own Gen Z team; at one point, he confesses that one member of his team actually quit instead of asking for a raise, which is an inherently "uncomfortable" conversation.
(https://www.youtube.com/watch?v=GON5fNGoDPk)

This is one of the deep dark secrets of Gen Z: they don't know how to deal with their own discomfort.

Where does this come from? It's hard to know (I'm not a psychologist), but I suspect over-protective parents don't help. Some Gen Z have parents who have done everything possible to keep their children from being in difficult situations.

I've heard of one CEO who actually had a mother show up with her child for an interview; when he asked why she was there, she said she wanted to be sure her child was in positive environment. "I said the interview was over," he said.

Many Gen Z are not familiar with the concept of being in an uncomfortable place, such as receiving feedback on their performance (if it's at all negative), disagreeing with a colleague, or not receiving something they want (bonus, promotion, raise, etc.).

Remember: many would rather quit than ask for a raise, they'd rather ghost someone than end a relationship face-to-face, and they'd rather complain online than confront their manager in a difficult situation.

3. They avoid conflicts - again, at all costs.

As a corollary of #2, one of the situations that Gen Z avoids is conflict, probably because they've not had good role-modeling for conflict resolution.

Think about it: when they've seen people argue, typically, it's been virtual (think Facebook, Reddit, and other social media channels). These discussions never end in a positive way and often devolve into name-calling or other bad behavior.

Conflict can take place in a number of ways, and Gen Z will avoid all these, so be on the lookout for these types of conflict at work:

- Not getting along with co-workers
- Not liking a manager
- Having issues with senior management decisions or policies

What can this conflict-avoidance look like? One is passive aggressive behavior, such as skipping team meetings or keeping the screen off on Zoom calls.

Please note: there may also be good reasons for this type of behavior that has nothing to do with conflict avoidance – these are just some of the signs that there may be a conflict issue that a younger worker is avoiding, rather than solving, because they don't know how to solve it.

4. They need constant feedback.

This isn't necessarily a deep dark secret - if you have younger employees - as they are often quite vocal about wanting feedback. The issue at hand is how often they want it; for some managers, it feels like an ongoing/daily/almost hourly concern.

Why do they seem to need this? It may stem from the way they were graded in school, where they received hourly feedback on how they were doing, from gold stars to good grades to awards.

Whatever the reason, it's something to keep in mind when hiring and onboarding a younger hire. They may demand more of your attention than you are used to, such as asking for 1:1 meetings on a weekly (if not daily) basis.

5. They are not resilient.

It seems paradoxical that this generation, which experienced both the 2008 economic crisis and the global pandemic, is not resilient. But it may be because of these two events that they are less resilient than other generations.

What are some examples of this?

- They have difficulty coping with, and bouncing back from, a failed project or task
- They don't know how to behave "in the moment" that something bad happens, such as hearing the news that they will not get a promotion or a raise
- Their inability to cope with negative feedback

One of your tasks, as a manager, will be to help them to be more resilient. This might be sharing, with them, how others have coped and done well in these types of situations, or modeling this type of behavior for them.

6. They are risk averse.

As a corollary to their lack of resilience, Gen Z tends to be risk averse. This means they may be fearful of being given a difficult assignment, or a task that is new to them. They may tend to want to have a routine that they can understand and follow, rather than being left on their own to manage their time.

Of course, growth typically comes from taking risks and doing new things that generate discomfort, so this type of behavior can keep younger employees from growing and learning. It will be incumbent on you, as their manager, to encourage them to take more risks and try new ideas, and to show them they need to do this in order to move forward in their careers.

One way to do this is to ensure that failure isn't punished (inaction is punished, instead). This will help to motivate those who have good ideas to try them, if they know that the repercussions for failing are not to their detriment.

7. They have difficulty thinking for themselves - and often lack critical thinking skills.

I've heard this frustration from senior management many times: "they don't think for themselves, even when I tell them what to do, they keep asking me questions instead of just doing it or figuring it out for themselves."

This habit of wanting to be told what to do, rather than thinking about what to do, may have been learned in school, where students have been taught to be successful on tests rather than to think, test, and learn on their own. In the U.S, we may have our educational system to blame for this and, if we want change, we may have to start at the educational level.

That said - it may be our new reality that younger workers are not accustomed to thinking about how to do their work, and they want to be told exactly what to do, and how to do it. As a manager, your role will be getting them from this level to the next level, where they are more self-sufficient and don't need your oversight or constant input.

8. ... But they also question process.

The interesting follow-up to this question of "How do we do this?" is feedback, from them, that it makes no sense. Or there's a faster way. Or there's an app for that.

This is where I believe there are huge opportunities for us, as managers, to capitalize on Gen Z's facility with technology. What might that look like?

When questioned, "How do I do that?" you might offer: "Here's how I do it. I consider X,Y,Z, and then do A,B,C. If that works for you, feel free to do it that way. AND, if you think there's a faster or more efficient way to do this that I don't know about, let me know! We're always looking for ways to improve how we do things here."

Whenever I work with a Gen Z who questions the process, I give them the background on how we got to where we are, and why, and then open it up for them to find a better way. This answers their question (how did we get here?) and also empowers them to improve on it.

In addition, allowing Gen Z to question processes to the point of finding a better way shows that you respect when they think for themselves (going back to Point #7) and derives a benefit from their dependence on technology (Point #1).

If they can find a better process, you've now shown them respect and moved your business processes forward! This type of appreciation will also have the benefit of increasing their engagement with their work and the organizations.

9. They don't trust authority and have no brand or company "loyalty."

Unlike their older, Millennial counterparts, Gen Z has little brand loyalty - as consumers or as employees - and they have very little trust in authority. This comes from their life histories, which is why I shared the stories, in Chapter 1, of three different Gen Z ready for the workforce.

Did you notice that they all had tragic family repercussions as a result of the Great Recession? They watched as their parents, who had devoted their time and energy to companies, were let go or tossed aside; it was clear that the loyalty they felt to their employers was not reciprocated when times were tough.

Observing this, Gen Z saw that companies "are not to be trusted," and for that reason any sense of company loyalty doesn't exist. They see the workplace as a way to make a living, but not much more.

Yes, some of them want careers, and will work hard to "climb the ladder." But they'll be on the lookout for greener pastures someplace else and will most likely bolt if they don't feel appreciated or feel that they are not learning and growing in their careers.

Some of these younger employees don't want a career, however. They're not interested in "climbing the corporate ladder." They want to do their work, put in their time, and then leave. They're more interested in their lives outside of work. They have strict boundaries between work and their outside lives.

If you want to keep these employees, it's important to understand their mindset, so that you can set up the rewards and educational opportunities appropriately.

10. They insist in "personal boundaries."

The corollary to having no brand or company loyalty is insisting on personal boundaries. As mentioned above, there are some Gen Z who want to do the work, put in the hours, and then leave. And they have strict boundaries between work and their outside lives. For them, the job ends as soon as they walk out the door.

And for those who are interested in careers, there's also an emphasis on personal boundaries. For example, Gen Z sees no reason to stay late at work - later than described in their job description - or to "go out after work" with colleagues.

While Gen Z appreciates face-to-face interactions, often more than their older Millennial colleagues, they sometimes feel that socializing with their colleagues is just more work. One of the best ways to get Gen Z to show up for an "after hours" social event is to do it during work hours. Otherwise, they'll more likely leave and do what they were planning to do - go to the gym, etc.

Now that you're aware of the 10 Deep Dark Secrets of Gen Z, let's move to the next step and understand how to use this background to interview and hire Gen Z.

The Secret to Managing Gen Z: The Handbook

Chapter 4 – What's Different About Interviewing and Hiring Gen Z

There are extensive books, written by Human Resource professionals, on how to *find* the best young talent. My goal here is to share with you best practices to use *when interviewing and hiring Gen Z* that will help you to be more successful in these efforts.

Here are the **ten steps you can do right now** to impact the success of your hiring the ideal Gen Z candidates.

1. Be brutally honest in your Job Descriptions

What do I mean by "brutally honest"? I mean write out exactly what you expect from your Gen Z hire once they're hired. Detail the things that you've thought that "people will come to understand once they're here."

That includes what hours you expect them to work, not the typical "9:00 – 5:00" but everyone is expected to stay until 5:30, or 6:00, or to stay until their manager or supervisor leaves.

Whenever I suggest this, someone always says, "but if we say that they won't take the job." And my response is, "If telling them this up-front means they don't take the job, then you've gotten rid of the wrong candidate quickly so you can move on to the right candidate."

This also means spelling out expectations about when you assume them to respond to email, or Teams messages, or Slack. First, you get to tell them that they're expected to respond to ALL the channels you use. Second, you get to tell them that they'll be expected to answer emails or messages up until 8:00 pm at night, or on weekends, or on Sunday evenings - if that's the case.

Or, even better, you tell them that they're NOT expected to respond to emails or texts unless it's urgent, and that you respect their personal boundaries. That will go a long way to attracting the right candidates.

Unless it's not true, in which case you've accomplished the same goal as mentioned above. If people are not willing to do what's expected of them – like returning emails in the evening, etc. -- then they're not the right candidate for the position.

And if this means that it's impossible to find the right people to fill the jobs, perhaps the hiring manager will change the way his or her team operates.

2. Spell out what your culture is – and your organization's values.

Does your organization value facetime in the office or getting the work done independently and remotely? I hear you saying "both" but, in reality, you either trust your employees or you don't. If you trust them, then you're okay with them not being in the office all the time.

You may ask, "How can I trust them when so many of them are taking vacations when I don't even know about it? I've seen it online, you say, they're off somewhere on a beach." My response to such questions is this: "Why do you care where they are, as long as the work gets done?"

There's the "real value" for you: the work gets done. No matter where the employees are. If it's high-quality work that doesn't need to be redone, isn't that a value your organization can stand behind?

What other values can you stand by that will appeal to Gen Z?

- Showing how every person in the organization makes a difference and contributes to the whole mission.
- Supporting everyone, in every role, from entry level to senior leadership.
- Educating everyone along their career journey, so they are "up to date" in all their skills, from tech to people skills and about the industry.
- Supporting your local community

These are just some of the values you can articulate to your employees and employment candidates; there are many others, too.

Read what your Glassdoor reviews say about you – and make some changes.

If you want to feel humbled, read your Glassdoor reviews. I worked at Pitney Bowes for years and was interested to see what was written about the company.

The Secret to Managing Gen Z: The Handbook

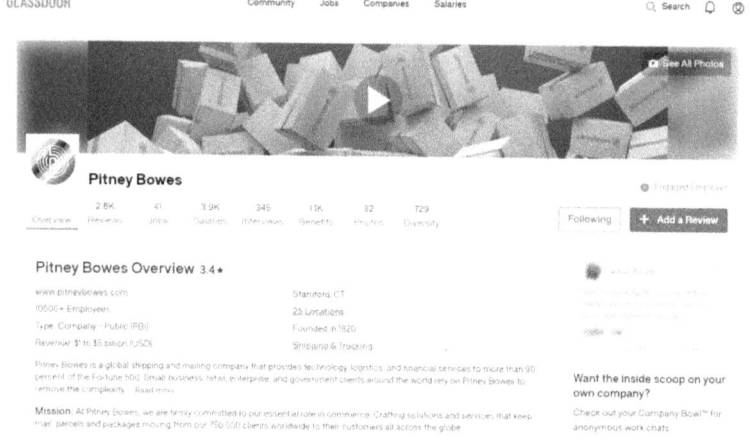

Summarizing the Pros and Cons of employee reviews:

Pros

- "Benefits are good and right" (in 225 reviews)
- "At my position I enjoyed the challenge was paid well and worked with great people." (in 201 reviews)

Cons

- "Management is poor is you are not a favorite" (in 127 reviews)
- "Poor upper Management who forgets who the little people are and are more concerned with how to make money." (in 58 reviews)

Are you aware of your reputation on Glassdoor? It may be influencing who comes through your door, when it comes to interviewing and onboarding. Anything that can influence potential employees should be assessed and reviewed; it's worth taking a good look at your reputation, as well as what you're doing for your employees.

3. Do Gen Z exit interviews.

One of the most valuable tools employers can use is the exit interview, because people are far more likely to tell you what they really think as they're walking out the door than if they are fearful for their jobs or careers.

Exit Interviews can be particularly helpful to find out:

- If there are specific team managers who need training or help managing their teams.
- If the organization is hiring the right "fit" for jobs.
- What issues or topics continue to come up as themes.

If you're not asking employees for their feedback as they're walking out the door, you're missing key insights into your organization.

4. Create a Career Advancement Plan: internal pathing and exploration.

Many Gen Z are more likely to stay with a company that promotes from within and offers opportunities to take on responsibility and upskill them. Do you have a clear pathway established for all your employees?

Depending on where you hire Gen Z in your organization, the pathing may be different. However, if you're a small organization and you're hiring young employees right out of school, it might be a good idea to set up an internal program that moves first-time employees around the organization.

Corporations used to do this, years ago, and called it "management training." They'd hire college graduates and move them around the company, giving them time to learn what goes on in various departments - from operations to customer service. This gave new employees a sense of how the company worked and what customers expected.

What typically happens, when younger employees have this experience, is:

- They are engaged because they're learning all the time.
- They can contribute "out of the box" ideas and solutions, coming in as outsiders.
- They learn how the business works.
- They make valuable contacts within the organization, for future projects and networking opportunities.

Over time, they find the area that is the best fit for them and, typically, they stay in this area and are promoted. This is still a great way to attract - and retain - new Gen Z employees. If you don't yet have an internal plan for your new hires, I suggest setting one up, and then talking about it during your interview process. It might make the difference to a potential new hire.

5. **Promote financial stability and offer perks.**

Gen Z - more than previous generations - has suffered from financial instability, thanks to the phenomena of COVID-19, the financial crisis of 2008, and crushing student loans. For that reason, they are very interested in financial perks and financial stability.

What are some of the ways you can help them in this area?

- Offer a competitive salary and share competitive data to illustrate how you're a fair employer.
- Offer health insurance that meets their needs - including mental health assistance.
- Offer services or refer employees to financial consultants, who can help them to manage their personal finances.
- Explore personal loan options that might be arranged, to help first-time employees with the expenses of living on their own - such as car loans or discounted rates.
- Create partnerships with local businesses to generate employee discounts, which creates the win-win of sending them your business and lowering employee expenses.

Whatever you can do to help Gen Z with their current financial burden will be appreciated, and will probably generate more interest in them working for your than your competition.

6. **Be up-to-date with both internal and external technology.**

Is your organization up-to-date with its use of technology? If you don't have the latest and greatest software or hardware, are you at least current within the last three years?

If the answer is 'no' to either of these questions, it will be tougher for you to recruit and retain talented Gen Z. As a generation, they've grown up with tech and they are sophisticated users of it. They expect to have it everywhere they go – and that includes the office.

There's another good reason for you to be keeping up with tech: if you don't, you'll be left behind by your competitors, who are keeping up and harnessing Gen Z talent to their advantage.

If you'd like to get back in the game, why not create a project for your organization around research and finding the best tech for the next five years? Assembling a multi-generational team for that project - utilizing the talent you have or may hire from Gen Z - is an ideal way to start.

7. Do you have a positive work culture? With some lifestyle flexibility?

Gen Z craves positive interactions and a social work culture, so one of the best ways to attract new Gen Z talent is to create a culture they'd like to join.

The first action you can take is to understand the work culture that you currently have. Do employees enjoy being part of teams? Do they get along with their managers? Do they have a positive experience during their workday?

If you've taken any of the actions I've recommended, you've already looked at your Glassdoor reviews. While these aren't always totally accurate, they can be directionally helpful. If culture came up as a problem, note that **culture starts at the top.**

That's good news! Because it means that you have the power to change it. Starting today, work on creating a culture that is good for employees, including first-line management. Give them all the support and training that they need to provide a good experience for those they supervise.

It starts with you. The way you manage will be reflected on down the line. Do you empower your direct reports? For example, how you deal with dissent determines whether you get a wide range of thoughts and opinions.

Finally, it's becoming trite to talk about work-from-home and many have written about the positive effects of offering this option - one, two, or three days a week - to employees. Be sure that you're staying current with the practice of empowering employees to be in charge of getting their work done. By doing so, you'll find you attract and retain the best employee talent.

8. **Is your leadership onboard with understanding Gen Z?**

Does everyone in a leadership position understand what it's like to work with Gen Z? That is, how to hire and gain from their insights and talent? And how to support them in their areas of weakness or concern?

If not, be sure that each one of them reads this book! It will provide them a framework for working with this new, talented generation, and for providing the support that everyone (of all ages) needs in the workplace.

I also recommend that you set up monthly or quarterly leadership meetings to discuss issues that have come up with younger employees. This shouldn't be a "complaint session" but rather a discussion of what issues have arisen and how they were dealt with successfully.

This becomes an internal way of sharing best practices, and can open many managers' eyes to the creative possibilities of resolving these issues in a way that benefits everyone in the organization.

If you don't have an internal facilitator who can set these up for you, hire someone from outside. Their job will be to:

- set up the agenda

- organize the meeting - who comes, where it is, communications, etc.
- collect stories ahead of time from volunteers
- lead the meeting in a way that ensures each manager shares his/her success story, answering questions, so that the entire organization moves forward in this area

[Not sure how to do this? Contact me – janet@janetgranger.com - so I can help.]

9. **Does your organization promote diversity of thought? Gen Z believes in diversity.**

DEI (Diversity, Equity, and Inclusion) has received quite a bit of backlash lately. Diversity as a premise at work stands for all types of diversity; for Gen Z, it includes *diversity of age*.

There's nothing more disheartening for a new, young employee than being very excited to be part of an organization and to try to contribute, only to find out your voice isn't heard - or, in many cases, wanted. When this happens, it leads to disengagement, apathy, and in many cases losing that employee in the next few months or year.

What are the advantages of having a younger voice in the group? I've used this example in Chapter 2, about the **church banners** representing Worship, Teaching and Friendship. To Gen Z and Millennials, the acronym spelled out at the top, as each banner has the letters boldly outlined, is WTF. To them, this popular acronym, reads "what the f**k?"

If the person or group at this organization had involved at least one younger person in the process of designing these banners - or even just the order in which they were displayed - this mistake could have been avoided.

To me, this says that whoever created this display was an older group that didn't acknowledge or reach out to younger people - perhaps those they were trying to attract - to ask them how the banners and message resonated with them.

Don't be this organization! Include your younger employees in your planning, whether it's about messaging, or your product, or even your goals.

This example illustrates so clearly why having multi-generational representation in any working group is critical. That's the DEI message here: the more people of different backgrounds and perspectives you involve in a project, the more diversity of approach you'll have. This will mitigate making mistakes and will, in many cases, propel you into interesting new areas of thought you may not have explored before.

How does this tie back to interviewing and hiring Gen Z? A younger employee who feels involved in the operations of your organization can become a great advocate for you. You can ask them to speak with younger candidates, to share "what it's like to work here." If they have a great story to tell, it will go a long way in helping you to hire more talent like them.

Chapter 5 – What's Different About Onboarding and Training Gen Z

As I've said in previous chapters, there is a great deal of expertise available in the HR world about how to onboard and train employees. You may have internal staff that does a great job now of onboarding and training.

This chapter is about how to be sure that these approaches include Gen Z, taking into account what makes them different from other generations.

In truth, I could spend days sharing stories about what Gen Z doesn't know and how bringing them into an organization differs now versus ten years ago. But I'll share some of the more obvious truths I've learned and, hopefully, that will open up some ideas for you - and your staff - about how to better manage bringing younger people into your organization.

1. **Be clear about dress code – what's acceptable and what isn't.**

Many in Gen Z didn't spend time in college learning about how to leave their rooms or their homes. As a result, they don't have as much practice as older generations - even Millennials - about what's expected in group settings. It's important to forgive them for 'not knowing' some of the basics when it comes to leaving their homes; and dress code is just one of these areas.

From the Gen Z perspective, if you've been able to attend class in your pajamas, simply by opening your laptop and logging on, in the comfort of your bed, you may not have received the proper messaging about appearances. No matter what your parents say - what do they know? they've been out of it for 20 years - and you've navigated life just fine in your sweats, shorts, and workout clothes.

While it may take some getting used to, it's important to start your onboarding process with the basics of what attire is deemed acceptable in your workplace. You might even want to include this in your acceptance letter, so it's clear from the beginning with each new employee what they're expected to wear at work.

This isn't the place for us to review what your particular workplace dress code is – that's up to you. What's important is that you:

- Write it down/codify it, so there are no mistakes.
- Share it with every employee at least once a year.
- Share it with new employees before they come to their first day of work.
- Stick to the code and ensure that exceptions are not allowed - otherwise, why have a code?

Again, there are plenty of HR people with experience that can share more about this; the learning for you is that this is an issue and the best way to deal with it is to be up-front about it as soon as the employee is hired.

2. Be clear about behavior that is acceptable in the workplace – such as drug use.

Here are some recent statistics about drug use in the workplace (*Source - https://newsroom.questdiagnostics.com/2024-05-15-Workforce-Drug-Test-Cheating-Surged-in-2023,-Finds-Quest-Diagnostics-Drug-Testing-Index-Analysis-of-Nearly-10-Million-Drug-Tests*)

*Drug positivity in the general U.S. workforce was **5.7%** in both 2022 and 2023. In 2023, in the combined U.S. workforce, urine drug positivity for all drugs was 4.6%, the same as in 2021 and 2022.* ***This overall positivity is the highest level in more than two decades, up more than 30% from an all-time low of 3.5% in 2010-2012,*** *and coincides with a sharp increase of 114.3% in post-accident positivity between 2015 and 2023 in the general U.S. workforce.*

There's a lot of scholarly research on why this has happened; I'm sharing these statics here to let you know what the general trend is so that you are aware.

If 6% of the U.S. workforce is testing positive for drugs and you have 100 employees - that means that, statistically speaking, there's a chance you have a handful of people who are on some type of drugs in the workplace.

If that's unacceptable to you, I suggest that you make your drug policy clear to all employees, current and prospective, on a regular basis - quarterly or yearly. Again, while you may have thought this was obvious to employees, it may not be to current generations.

When I spoke to a Vistage group in South Florida, one CEO complained to the group that he used a part-time staffing agency for his warehouse operations, and he was appalled to find that many of his workers were going out into the parking lot during work hours to get high, then coming back inside to work.

As you might imagine, this created a dangerous work environment not only for those who were high but also for those who were not.

Even if you don't believe this is a problem for you, I recommend that you head this potential issue off at the pass - as they used to say in Westerns - and make sure that your drug use policy is stated

- loud and clear - on a regular basis - for all employees. That starts with the onboarding process and continues with ongoing training.

3. What time does the job start – unofficially and officially – and when does it end?

Are the hours from the job description accurate when it comes to the real role and management expectations? I asked this question back in Chapter 2, about what the expectations were for the job and said that one of the first, best ways to affect the attraction of younger employees is to be honest about this.

When it comes to onboarding and training, being clear about the parameters of job expectations is better than taking a more nuanced approach. In fact, it can even help with management training, so that managers can be clear about their expectations and more empathetic when employees run into difficulties in their personal lives that conflict with their workplace attendance or responsibilities.

Here are a few examples of ways to onboard younger employees when it comes to the parameters of their roles:

- How often will they be expected to be in the office? And why?
- What is the preferred mode of internal communication? (Teams, Slack, email, etc.)
- What is the expectation for returning internal communications after hours?
- What is the expectation for returning internal communications on the weekends?
- What is the expectation for returning internal communications when on PTO?

Further communications about when they are expected to be in the office or online might include:

- Will their manager and teammates be in the office at the same time? If not, why not?
- How far in advance do they need to plan their vacation/PTO?

Finally, this might also pique your thoughts about exceptions that might be made for these rules when "life gets messy." These might include sharing:

- What accommodations are available for families?
- What accommodations are made for mental health?

Hopefully, these suggestions illustrate that it's best to be clear, at the outset, what is expected from a new employee so that there are fewer misunderstandings.

4. Are activities "outside the workplace" important? Why?

Many organizations approach the question of culture with the idea of creating a "team" feeling between employees through activities that are outside the normal workplace. This might include off-site retreats, volunteering days - think "Habitat for Humanity" volunteer teams - or the informal going-out-for-drinks-after-work.

Speaking as a woman who worked in corporate America both as a single person and then while raising children, I will say that some of these worked well for me and some did not. When I was young and single and living in NYC, the days of corporate outings to a baseball game were fun and exciting. We'd all pour out of the building, board the subway, and spill into the stadium as a group, laughing and sharing throughout the afternoon and evening.

These outings, like the Corporate Run in Central Park, were fun events and I appreciated them, discovering good friendships at work because of them.

However, after I was married and had small children, I found my ability and inclination to share in these types of activities diminished. When I wasn't working, I was eager to spend time with my family. And, on top of that, I became resentful when companies expected me to extend my work time into my personal time, doing an activity that was "work-related."

The best examples of these activities were when the organization acknowledged that families and children existed and, instead of competing with them, added them into the mix. For example, I worked for a private company that had an event every year around Halloween, inviting all the employees' children to "come to work" dressed up. They hosted talent, like magicians, to entertain everyone, and provided snacks.

I was always impressed that those who didn't have young children would also attend these events, to get a glimpse of the kids and to share in their colleagues' "outside lives." (Imagine being able to say hello to your boss's children, or even entertain them for a moment of fun.)

I remember asking one older employee, on the facilities team, why he attended these parties (he was a grandfather at the time), and he said he just got a kick out of watching the kids and seeing how people acted with their families; they often seemed more relaxed and happy than they appeared during a normal workday.

Was the Halloween party mandatory? Absolutely not. Was it "life enhancing" for me and my kids? Absolutely. They got to see my workplace, meet my colleagues, and have fun at the same time. I got to meet other families and see my colleagues as more well-rounded people than the professional versions of themselves I saw at work all the time.

Why am I sharing all this? Because asking people to attend "company events" or "team events" outside of the workplace can and should be something that every employee wants and looks forward to, but they are not. For introverts like me, the idea of "hanging out" with my colleagues often inspires more dread and stress than a desire to "bond."

I share this because the planning of extracurricular activities is often done by extraverts for extraverts, without taking into consideration how painful it can be for those who are not energized by the company of other people. Consider all these factors when planning company events that are outside the workplace or work hours:

- How will this feel for introverts?
- Will parents with young children be able to attend without having to find daycare?
- Will people who work remotely attend? Will accommodations be made for them?
- Are you setting a standard that those who don't have children or other outside commitments are "favored"?

Based on all this, my recommendation is always to have these types of events during normal business hours, as this makes it easiest for everyone to attend, and to bring in those working outside the office for these events.

5. What are the communication channels everyone should use?

It's important to make it clear, during an onboarding or orientation process, that certain lines of communication are expected. It doesn't matter what these are, just that your organization is explicit and clear about what channels everyone should use.

For example, if your organization uses the Microsoft suite of products, you might want to be sure everyone is on Teams. That's for internal communications - chats and messaging - as well as for meetings.

Why is this important? Because it's frustrating for everyone if people are looking for messages on a channel, like Teams (or Slack), while some employees are sending out internal communications via email.

The only aspect of this which is more frustrating - and comical, sometimes - is the "reply all" button that gets used for emails. This leads to an incredible amount of time being wasted while people are reading and tracking an internal email that should have been a post. (Think birthday messages, notices about a meeting, or even thank-you's that get sent out to dozens of people.)

One of the great aspects of these internal communication tools is that they can be customized: you can create groups of teams, so that people don't receive messages that aren't relevant for them. Also, it means that emails are typically from outside the organization, so they don't build up and they can be reviewed more quickly.

Let all new employees know what channels are to be used internally, and how they are to be used, so that everyone is using the correct channels. This will ensure communication flows internally as it's supposed to. And it ensures that important external communications are seen promptly.

One final note: if you hold online meetings, such as Teams, and the expectation is that everyone will be "on screen" - with their cameras on - this should be made clear at the outset. This might lead back to another discussion about how one should appear onscreen. For example, are you expected to be upright - at a desk or at a table - rather than lying in bed?

Questions like this might seem silly, but remember that many older Gen Z went to school or were in college during the pandemic; they could have been in bed in their pajamas while attending class online.

To make the transition from schooling to a work environment, all new employees should be told how they are expected to "show up" onscreen, just as they need to know the 'in-person' dress code. A brief class on the best way to be onscreen - highlighting backgrounds that are appropriate, lighting that works best, sound that is optimal, etc.- are also appropriate for this discussion.

6. **Be clear about paid-time-off: what's the policy and how is it used?**

It's important to be as clear about what PTO means for everyone in the organization as it is to be clear about #3, what are the real hours and days you're expected to work. What do I mean by that?

Answer for each employee the following questions:

- "Am I expected to leave my **notifications on in our internal channel (Slack, Teams, etc.) in case you need me for something important?**" I'm hopeful that the answer is no here: nothing is so important - unless you're a senior level manager - that you need to be "on call" while on vacation.

- **How far in advance of the PTO does your manager need to be notified?** A day? A month? Three or six months? Be explicit about how much time a manager needs in order to be sure there's coverage, if necessary.

- o **Do you get your desired PTO or do you "apply" for it – with your manager giving final approval on the dates?** Examples: for sales, during the end-of-year push to close, who gets to take time off for the holidays? Let new employees know how this works, so they're prepared for the process.

These examples show the type of explicit wording that should be clear to new employees, so they do all the right notifications in order to get the PTO they deserve.

There may be more issues that come up in your organization, during the orientation or onboarding process. These are some of the "hot buttons" that are important to Gen Z, so be sure that these particular topics are covered.

Chapter 6 – How to Keep Gen Z Employees

Now that you've changed many of your internal processes to attract and onboard Gen Z talent, it's important to generate a return-on-investment for your hard work and spend by keeping them at your company.

What's the secret to retaining the best young talent? Deliver on what you've promised them. It sounds rather plain and simple, but it's not. In some cases, that means keeping a careful check on your internal culture, ongoing training for managers, and being on the lookout for potholes in your organization and processes where young talent can fall in and get trapped.

Understand the "brain science" of being human – and how it motivates younger employees – and their managers

In my previous book, I spent some time outlining the brain science behind human motivation. If you haven't read it, I'm repeating those learnings again. (If you have read it already, feel free to skip to the next section, 1. Provide Ongoing Feedback).

Let's start with recent discoveries about human brain. Back in 1994, Antonio Damasio, a neuroscientist, stumbled upon an interesting fact about the decision-making part of the human brain. He studied various people who had damage in the part of the brain where emotions are generated. He found that these people seemed "normal" in every way, except that they didn't feel any emotions.

And they all had another trait in common: they couldn't make decisions.

This was novel and ground-breaking. Consider: whenever you make a decision based on "facts" - *you aren't really making that decision based on facts*. You're making a decision based on a "gut feeling," or you're leaning in one direction or another based on an emotion.

This makes sense when people talk about "just having a feeling" about something, and "going with their gut." What they sensed was the emotions they had swaying them in one direction versus another and they trusted what they were feeling. Even if it meant that they were going against what the "facts" were telling them.

If you consider yourself a data hound (like me!) who focuses only on facts and data, consider that you collect and review enough data to "make yourself feel comfortable" with making a decision. If you haven't seen enough data, or it is conflicted, you'll keep going until you "feel confident" about making a decision.

This also explains why people of different backgrounds or political persuasions don't seem to be swayed by what their opponents, or others, refer to as "the facts;" instead, a person's decision-making process seems to be set, or highly influenced, by the emotions that the decision creates or fosters. This has huge implications in many areas and industries.

In 2010, an article in *Psychology Today* outlined the connection between emotion and logic, and how what one might refer to as "logical decisions" are predominantly molded by emotions. "Emotions have tremendous action potential. Yet the drive that emotions provide, particularly in the workplace, is sometimes experienced as stress related..."

Or, as the article's title says, "like it or not, emotions will drive the decisions you make today."

Primary Emotions

There's an interesting TED talk by scientist Natasha Sharma, who reveals how our emotions drive our daily decisions. She says we make approximately 35,000 decisions in one day. She then notes that people don't take care of their "emotional health" and "emotional fitness" the way they take care of their physical fitness, or mental fitness (doing crossword puzzles, for example). As youngsters, we're not taught how to deal with our emotions.

She says that people associate conventional wisdom with success and happiness in life. But people who show higher levels of "emotional fitness" are - in her studies and others - more likely to be happier and successful in later life.

Emotional fitness is going to be critical going forward, she says, because of the rate of change going on in the world right now. Our mental ability to deal with this rapid pace of change, and a faster, more automated world, has not changed, however, so we are not all as able to "keep up." And this means that people are becoming more stressed, and having more anxiety. It will be more crucial than ever for people to be able to manage their emotions.

This is particularly true for younger people, who are dealing with many stressful situations in life. Consider: the average income for people age 18 - 35 has gone down for the past 25 years, while the cost-of-living has increased (Natasha gave this TED talk in 2017, long before the Coronavirus stopped the world and more young adults, age 22 – 25, found themselves unemployed than ever before).

She goes on to note that the majority of jobs being created are part-time or contract. Meanwhile, student debt is the highest it's ever been, and wealth disparity in the U.S. is the highest it's ever been.

Of all the emotions, she notes, there are only three that matter the most when it comes to driving our decision-making processes: love, hate and fear.

Natasha asserts that, at some point in our lives, we will feel as though "someone has wronged us" and they have to "pay for it."

Feelings of hate and anger keep us "stuck" on that idea, so it's important to let those emotions go. And the only way to eradicate those emotions is to change our expectation of the world as a "just and equal place" - because it's not.

Sometimes life is not fair; sometimes, people hurt us. This is part of the human experience, so if individuals can learn how to come to terms with these emotions, and reach the realization that 'life is not fair,' they will be able to let go of fear and hate.

The implications in the work environment are many: we're afraid of failure, we're afraid of not being acknowledged or appreciated, we're afraid of getting hurt, we're afraid of the unknown. We're afraid of many things, including losing our jobs/livelihood.

"Your emotions rule," she notes, "so learn to rule your emotions," she advises.

Implications in the workplace

Let's think about the implications this knowledge has on how we look at the workplace. In 2007, Wharton professor Sigal Barsade, an award-winning researcher/teacher who studies the influence of emotions in the workplace wrote, "Emotions travel from person to person like a virus."

"The state of the literature shows that affect matters because people are not isolated 'emotional islands.' Rather, they bring all of themselves to work, including their traits, moods and emotions, and their affective experiences and expressions influence others," according to the paper, co-authored by Donald Gibson of Fairfield University's Dolan School of Business.

She suggests that "while some people are better than others at controlling their emotions, that doesn't mean their coworkers aren't picking up on their moods. 'You may not think you are showing emotion, but there's a good chance you are in your facial expression or body language. Emotions we don't even realize we are feeling can influence our thoughts and behaviors."

People "bring all of themselves to work, including their traits, moods and emotions, and their… experiences and expressions influence others."

For that reason, it's important to consider what it means to have all these emotions playing out in the workforce, all day long.

If a worker (young or older) believes that life should be fair, for example, and is fearful of losing her position, it can make her miserable. Layer that with other issues - she's not feeling respected at work by her colleagues, and she isn't getting the funding she needs, from her boss, for her team and their work - and it is understandable now why younger workers can get so upset; fear creates a highly stressful situation.

Emotions are not acknowledged at work because emotion is a value-laden word.

Looking at this research, it's clear that there are emotions playing out in the workplace - because we're all human. But there's an important contradiction: there's no place for emotions in the workplace.

"Emotion *affects so many parts of work, from collaboration to decision-making, motivation, and communication between employees and managers. But in American culture, 'emotional' can be a dirty word. There's a misconception that expressing feelings is unprofessional or out of place in the office.*"

If you ask Baby Boomers and Gen Xers, who are often the senior management and leaders in organizations, whether they're being emotional, perhaps sending emotional signals to others, they may deny it. They have been brought up to believe that emotion has no place at work – but that's only because they don't acknowledge that it's happening all around them, all the time, including amongst themselves. Yet everyone picks up on these signals, in body language or spoken words, consciously or unconsciously.

Each organization has its own emotional culture. What's yours?

If you're not sure, you can get a sense from answering this question: what's a story that you can tell - about your organization - that would "only happen there?"

One example, from IDEO's New York studio, is that one day a week, their lunches are "dedicated to Make(believe) time." This allows employees to explore their creativity, even if it sounds silly or goofy. Other signals might be silly GIFs that circulate the office, or idiosyncratic messaging from senior management.

Why is the emotional culture important at work? Because when employees feel supported (and motivated) by their colleagues, they are happier and will stay in the organization longer - and they are probably more productive, too. Most importantly, it helps employees to deal with stresses better and to trust their colleagues and management more.

All this leads to a better working environment for everyone.

Emotions are there – even if they're not appreciated or acknowledged.

What happens in the workplace if everyone is acting out of his/her own emotional intelligence and personal state, but it's not being acknowledged? And, in fact, people are told to keep their emotions out of their decision-making?

There's a perpetuation of the myth that everything that happens in the office is fact-based, merit-based, and fair. It's going the way it should be. When, in reality, it's not that way at all.

In reality, as Natasha Sharma noted, everyone is acting out of basic emotions: love, hate, and fear - with fear being the one that comes into play the most, in many work situations.

Back to why being human matters.

This is where science makes the work situation most interesting - specifically, understanding that *everyone* has emotions that are driving decision-making at work. Because all managers of teams are also dealing with their own emotions in their decision-making processes.

The beauty of understanding why and how humans work - how everyone acts and reacts in the work environment - is that the generalizations we make here apply universally. There are no exceptions to the rule, as happens so often with generalizations about age groups.

That said, we do need to take into account how individuals manage their emotions; that becomes unique and individual. But looking for and understanding the emotions in every person, at every level, is a great starting place for understanding what's going on – in teams, in organizations, etc.

I've met with senior management teams for many Gen Z and younger Millennials and this has provided a perspective on what goes on at the upper levels of management that affect younger teams. The most interesting – though not surprising – finding is that many managers act out of fear, also.

What fears do managers have? Here are just some of them:

- Fear of providing budget that is poorly spent.
- Fear of not getting results needed from a team - for the manager.
- Frustration that the team doesn't perform well.
- Fearful for the stability of one's own position.
- Reluctance to speak with the boss about team dynamics - because that conversation makes one look bad, as a manager.

As you can see, that's a lot of fear! It's no wonder that younger employees get stonewalled and frustrated.

Bridging the gap

There can be a huge chasm of communication, trust and understanding between younger teams and their management. How does one bridge that gap? It takes work on the part of managers and leadership.

While each case is different, in terms of the exact strategies and meetings, the goal is always the same: understanding that each generation - each individual - has her/his emotions at work. Clarifying what those emotions are and what decision-making they drive is key.

The best way to empower every generation in the workplace is to work with every individual, treating them as an individual, rather than dealing with classifications of age groups. This is a fundamentally - almost radically - different approach from others who teach how to resolve these issues in the workplace.

What's the best way to retain younger workers? To understand that this dynamic is going on all day, every day, and to empower managers with the skills and understanding to deal with it.

In addition to understanding the brain science around people dynamics and management, here are some additional steps to take to retain younger talent.

1. **Provide ongoing feedback.**

More than any previous generation, Gen Z craves ongoing, almost constant, feedback. Why? Most likely because they grew up at a time when most schools were focused on "teaching to the test." They were taught how to answer questions, not how to think about questions, or how to think for themselves.

One of the best ways to retain younger employees is to give them constructive, ongoing feedback and to be careful about the wording. It should be positive, appreciative of their efforts, and point out what they did well as well as where they can improve.

Most importantly, the feedback should include a statement about the individual's worth and potential, so they don't hear the feedback as affirmation that they're not good enough. You might say, "I know you can do this" or "I'm telling you this because I know you're the right person to do this."

If someone wants ongoing feedback, set up weekly or bi-weekly meetings to review with them what they are doing, how they are working and learning, and to provide guidance for growth.

2. **Provide a path for career advancement.**

For younger employees who are ambitious, Gen Z wants to know, at the outset, what a career path might look like at your organization.

One of the best ways to ensure that younger talent stays in your organization is to show them, at the outset, how that might work. For example, when hiring for an entry-level position, share that the next level in the organization requires:

- 2 – 3 years of experience in a working environment (such as yours)
- 2 – 3 years working with your industry
- 2 – 3 years working with other internal departments
- Proficiency in the software used in your department
- 2 years of experience performing and delivering work on-time, complete, without needing to be redone
- (etc.)

As noted earlier, formal Management Programs from the past made a practice of rotating employees into different areas of the organization. This ensured each employee had a sense of how all the departments worked together, as well as the particulars and special skills needed in each area.

You might want to create a program that rotates ALL employees (including younger ones) so that they find the best fit for their skills and gifts.

The bottom line is this: younger talent is more likely to stay with a company that promotes from within and offers opportunities to take on responsibility and upskill. Showing them what a path might look like, as well as establishing training programs to provide the skills and knowledge they need to advance, will help to retain your best talent.

3. Stress the need for ongoing communication.

Younger employees have a great fear of failure, and one common trait they have is shutting down in their communications when all is not well.

As a manager, your role is to let them know that this is not in their best interest. As an employee, being more communicative when you need help is better. Assure them that the best way to get the assistance and the guidance they need, especially when they're stumped or blocked or just feeling frustrated, is to ask.

On the topic of communication, it's critical that younger and new employees understand the channels that are used internally at your organization, as well as best practices for using them. For example, as mentioned earlier, if your company is using the Microsoft suite of products, including Teams - and Teams meetings - then be sure that employees know that they need to do all internal outreach on Teams.

Another great way to use internal communications is to make sure that younger employees know where to go when they have questions. If you don't provide resources, they'll simply Google answers as best they can when they don't know something.

Setting up an internal FAQ that's searchable by keywords is a great way to ensure that protocols are followed correctly and internal procedures and standards are adhered to.

4. Provide resources for mental health and ask "how are you doing?"

At a recent presentation on the topic of managing younger generations in the workplace, someone in sales asked me what she should do when team members complain of being "burned out" all the time.

It's a great question and made me want to include it here. Do you have younger employees who complain about being "burned out" all the time? If so, there are a couple of possible solutions:

1) They are not burned out by the job – something else is going on.
2) They are burned out by the job – which is a problem with their position.

It's easiest to help when they're not burned out by the job but by something else. For example, you might ask them, "what exactly is causing you to feel burned out?" You might be surprised by the responses.

For example, some people have stressful situations at home: issues with their parents, their partners, their children, feeling lonely, etc. If their personal situation is stressful, they don't have the opportunity to leave work and relax. Their "off" time is actually making life difficult.

If their personal lives are contributing to their stress, one of the best resources you can provide is a way for them to learn to cope. This means offering mental health services. What you can offer depends on your organization, of course. But having this conversation and making resources available will go a long way in retaining your younger talent.

5. Ask for technology suggestions to improve processes.

Leaders in every industry are doing their best to figure out how to leverage AI, and my advice to all of them is to involve younger employees in this work. For the most part, they've grown up with technology and use it all day, every day; why not take advantage of their comfort with it and their ability to find new ways to solve problems, do work, and improve processes?

Involving younger workers in the struggle to stay technologically relevant is one of the most efficient uses of your talent pool. In addition, it gives younger talent a pathway to feel as though they're appreciated and can add value to the organization.

In addition to AI, you might use your Gen Z talent to offer other ways to improve your use of technology. It's critical for them to understand how you got to where you are now. Here are just some of the questions you can have them learn and explore, to help you:

- What choices went into the current technology?
- What are the costs of changing – not just financially, but potential risk and downtime?
- What are the risks of *not* upgrading your tech?
- What is your competition doing in this area?

Workers of all ages can team to help your organization stay technologically relevant, and this is a great area to show how all ages can work together efficiently and effectively.

6. Encourage they take time off and vacation seriously.

On the other side of younger employees feeling "burned out" all the time is the risk that they be so fearful of not doing well, of not being promoted, or of not getting a raise that they don't take the time off that they should.

Take a look at the cartoon below. It gives you a great example of why Gen Z feels burned out. Older generations had no problems taking vacations and being "unplugged" before the internet. Now that's all changed.

The cartoon depicts an "out of office" message that explains in painful detail the inability for conscientious younger employees to be unplugged from office emails and messages. To add insult to injury for this employee, she ends with "in the meantime try my supervisor, Wendy, who's already made at me for taking time off."

Cartoon by Jeremy Nguyen August 2, 2024

When did we start resenting workers for taking their time off?

While some individuals may take advantage of time off, many will do the opposite because they're not used to work/life boundaries. Remember that this younger generation has always had their phones with them. They're used to being pinged every time there's a post on their Instagram, or someone texts them, etc. While this can create great dopamine hits, it can also cause stress if they're not allowed to stop answering emails and texts 24/7.

It's important to be sure that younger employees know that they do NOT have to check in while they're on vacation, at the doctor's office or in the hospital, or simply enjoying their weekend. Creating this boundary will allow them to relax and get the rest they need so they can be fresh and ready for work during the week.

As I mentioned above, someone in sales shared that her team members complained of being burned out all the time. When we discussed why that might be, she admitted that they were "on call" 24 hours a day and were expected to respond to sales inquiries as soon as possible.

No wonder they felt burned out! Can you imagine being at a job where you're expected to be "on" all the time? Even physicians who are "on call" at the hospital get a break so they can be rested enough to deal with life-and-death situations.

If your team is burned out and it's because you expect them to work all the time, I'd like to suggest that it's not their fault – it's the fault of their job or job description. Everyone needs to be able to rest, relax, and recharge.

In most industries, if you don't create a work environment in which younger employees have the opportunity to have breaks and time off, I predict that you'll have high turnover rates. And these, in turn, decrease your profitability, since you'll have to spend many more resources on attracting, interviewing, onboarding, and training new employees over and over again.

Now that we've covered how to keep younger Gen Z talent in the workplace, let's talk a bit about how and why Millennials (those in their 30's and early 40's) have risen to management positions so quickly, and what it means for managing teams of all ages.

Chapter 7 - Why So Many Millennials are in Leadership Positions

Why are so many Millennials in leadership positions? The short answer is: it's math.

Many Millennials (ages 28 – 41, as this book is written) find themselves in management and leadership roles now and have difficulty managing Gen Z. How did that happen? And why is it a struggle?

How we got here

We'll start with the how it happened first. And it comes down to the math around populations in the past 60 years. See the following chart, which outlines the size of each generation we've been talking about.

By the year 2035 (that is, within 10 years of this writing), the Baby Boom generation that was so large will be out of the workplace and Gen X will replace them as the "elders" in the workplace.

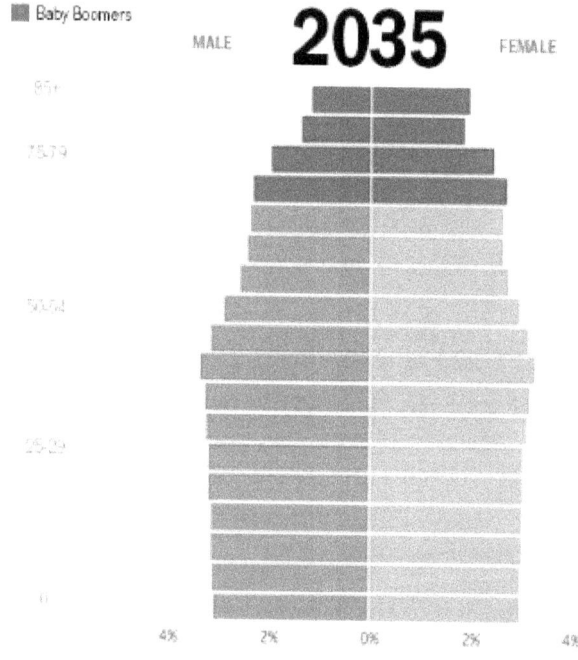

Gen X was born in the years 1965-1980. In 2025, they will be in the age range of 55 – 70. Looking at the sizes of the bars in the above graphic, you can see how the graph gets narrower in these age ranges.

On the other hand, Millennials (Gen Y), who were born from 1981-1996, will be in the age range of 39-54. Look at how the graph bulges out to the left and right for these age ranges. That's because this generation represents, for the most part, the children of the Baby Boomers. While there was a "bump" upwards in baby births after WWII, there was a similar "bump" in baby births as these babies had their own children.

In fact, the year 1990 represents that next biggest "boomlet" of baby births recorded after the Baby Boomers, with 4.16 million births recorded in that one year alone.
(https://www.thoughtco.com/baby-boom-overview-1435458)

Why does it matter?

Why all the detail about the size of the populations? Because it makes a difference in the workplace: someone has to do the work, and someone typically oversees the work. There are levels of responsibility and management in any organization.

Gen X is aging and has fewer people in it than the Boomers. The oldest Gen X, born in 1965, are getting towards retirement age. This will only accelerate over time. As they retire, there are more and more openings for senior management - taking for granted, for the moment, that people who are older are typically in more senior level positions. If Boomers and Gen X are both retiring, that leaves a gap in a healthy, growing economy.

That gap is starting to be filled by Millennials. Right now, the oldest Millennials are in their early 40's and they are starting to find themselves promoted up into senior level positions. Or they may now have their own small businesses.

This is why the math – how many births there were in each generation – is determining which generation finds itself in management and leadership positions.

Millennials are the biggest generation

Interestingly enough, Millennials comprise the largest share of the workforce at this writing (see graph below) at 35%. This will remain relatively constant, while the share of Gen Z in the workforce will be 30% by 2030. Gen X comprises 30% of the workforce because, again, there are fewer of them.

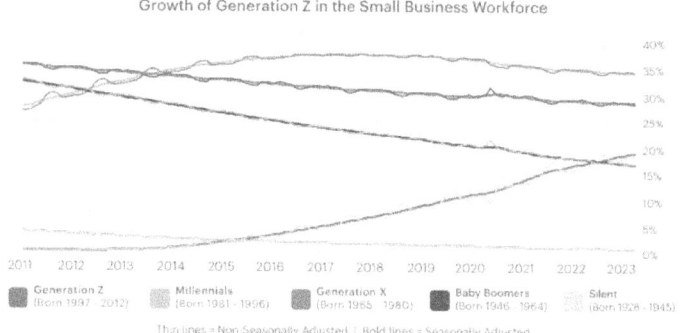

This book is about managing Gen Z and is written for ALL the generations, including Millennials. Those born in 1990, in their mid-30s, can be as confused about how to manage this younger generation as those who are in their mid-40s.

While more and more Millennials are finding themselves overseeing Gen Z, there are also Gen X senior directors and VPs who oversee first-level managers. This book is for everyone, to help understand what makes Gen Z tick and what makes them different from the generations who have come before.

Chapter 8 – A Brief Explanation of the Generation Framework

Why do we talk about the different generations in the first place? What does it matter?

For those who are looking for the academic framework that this theory hangs on, this is a brief summary of the study of Generations, which started in the 1990s with the book ***Generations: The History of America's Future, 1584 to 2069***, by William Strauss and Neil Howe.

In this groundbreaking book, the authors suggest the following theory of how people move through their lives, how they age (and think) over their lifetimes. If we think of our lives as one long track, like a railroad track, with birth as the "place of origin" and death as the "destination." They suggest that we "imagine phase-of-life stations along the way, from childhood to elderhood."

Now, picture a series of "generational trains, all heading down the track at the same speed. While one (generational) train is moving from one station to the next, other trains are also rolling down the track. If we picture ourselves sitting at any given station, watching one train go and another arrive, we notice how different each train looks from the next." (p.29)

What are they describing? What we now refer to as the different generations: Baby Boomers, Gen X, Millennials, and Gen Z.

The authors described how each generation is always aging, "moving up one lifecycle notch roughly every twenty-two years."

And, they note, "the behavior and attitudes of each phase of life change character entirely" from one generation to the next (p.31).

They study American history and assert: "Take any phase of life, move forward or backward a quarter century, and you will invariably discover profound changes in what it meant to be that age in America."

One great example, to think about this, is to consider what it was like to be a teenager in the 1950s, in post-WWII America, versus the 1960s, with the protests of the war in Vietnam and the rise of the "hippie" generation, to the 1970s with the rise of rock-and-roll and discretionary incomes among teens.

This is in contrast to 30 years later, in the 1980s, when teens were into recording their own music on cassette tapes, Walkman personal stereos, video games, and early home computers. The list goes on and on, and accelerates after the advent of personal computing and smartphones.

Looking at the teenage phase of life, you can see how being a teenager in the U.S. changed dramatically over time, from one generation to the next.

What is a Generation?

All of this leads to the authors defining what a generation is and why it's important. A "generation" is a "cohort-group whose length approximates the span of a phase of life and whose boundaries are fixed by peer personality." (p. 60)

The authors note that it's critical to understand the two important elements of any generation: the *length* of a generational cohort-group and its *peer personality*. (p.60)

What I find most interesting is how the authors have defined "peer personality," which they describe as the way "a generation collectively feels historical urgency and finality, conscious of the unrepeatable opportunities offered by whatever phase of life it occupies."

The definition is "a generational persona recognized and determined by (1) common age location; (2) common beliefs and behavior; and (3) perceived membership in a common generation." (p.63-64)

Much of what creates this peer personality occurs because of what the authors call "social moments: an era, typically lasting about a decade, when people perceive that historic events are radically altering their social environment."

Think about pivotal moments in your lifetime: the COVID 19 pandemic, for example, or the financial collapse of 2008. Other examples of these social moments include wars and scientific breakthroughs, such as landing a man on the moon in 1969.

The authors call these "secular crises, when society focuses on reordering the outer world of institutions and public behavior; and spiritual awakenings, when society focuses on changing the inner world of values and private behavior." (p.71)

Predicting the Crisis of 2020

This book was written in 1991, and what I found most impressive was their prediction, based on their theories, of a "Crisis of 2020." Based on their review of historical cycles, they wrote: "The climactic event may not arrive exactly in the year 2020, but it won't arrive much sooner or later." (p. 381)

The authors projected "a crisis lasting from 2013 to 2024," noting "the early 2020s appear fateful." (p.382) How significant with the crisis be, they asked themselves?

> *"Recall the parallel eras... the American Revolution, the Civil War, and the years spanning the Great Depression and World War II. The Crisis of 2020 will be a major turning point in American history and an adrenaline-filled moment of trial. At its climax, Americans will feel that the fate of posterity – for generations to come – hangs in the balance.*

What happened in 2020? Think about both the worldwide pandemic that hit the U.S. in March of that year, and the heated presidential election that followed in the fall. The election had its aftermath into 2021, with the storming of the U.S. Capitol on January 6, 2021. Their prediction seems to have played out, looking at how the American public is divided politically, and doesn't seem to have resolved itself as of 2024.

When do they predict that the turmoil will end? They believe that by 2030, American society will have "settled" into a new era. (p.383)

Generational theory lives on

Whether or not you believe in their version of the cyclical nature of history, their definitions of the various generations seem to have lasted in the decades since their book was published. While we use slightly different years and names to define the current generations, we still subscribe to the theory that groups of people all born in the same era, experiencing the same historical events and sharing the same memories as they age, tend to share similar values and exhibit similar behaviors.

The Secret to Managing Gen Z: The Handbook

In writing this book, I've been assuming the general framework of this generational theory. And now you know where it came from.

You now have a better sense of why many Gen Z act and think the way they do, and how we arrived at this particular time and place, from a generational perspective.

If you would like additional help with understanding and working with Gen Z, please reach out to me at janet@janetgranger.com.

Please also follow me on LinkedIn – my profile is here: https://www.linkedin.com/in/janetgranger/ - and check out my website: www.janetgranger.com for my blog posts and additional information.

Thanks so much for reading!

The Secret to Managing Gen Z: The Handbook

The Secret to Managing Gen Z: The Handbook

Selected Bibliography

The following is a curated list of the books and articles used to research this book.

1. AbodeHR. "2024 Gen Z Research." *AbodeHR*, 2024, https://assets-global.website-files.com/634473f9bd72042299aea7fb/65f1e77d703d899764a8dfde_2024GenZResearch.pdf

2. AbodeHR. "What You Need to Recruit and Retain Gen Z." *AbodeHR*, https://www.abodehr.com/blog/what-you-need-to-recruit-and-retain-gen-z

3. "Baby Boom Overview." ThoughtCo. https://www.thoughtco.com/baby-boom-overview-1435458

4. BambooHR. "How to Manage Generation Z." *BambooHR*, https://www.bamboohr.com/blog/how-to-manage-generation-z

5. Big Think. "Decisions Are Emotional, Not Logical: The Neuroscience Behind Decision Making." https://bigthink.com/personal-growth/decisions-are-emotional-not-logical-the-neuroscience-behind-decision-making/

6. Constine, Josh. "The Slack Origin Story." *TechCrunch*, 2019, https://techcrunch.com/2019/05/30/the-slack-origin-story

7. 7.Deloitte. "Help Me Grow: What Motivates Gen Z?" *Deloitte*, 2023, https://www2.deloitte.com/us/en/blog/business-chemistry/2023/help-me-grow-what-motivates-gen-z.html

8. DDI. "Frontline Leader Project Research eBook." *DDI*, https://media.ddiworld.com/research/frontline-leader-project_research_ebook_ddi.pdf

9. Gallo, Amy. "The Secret to Becoming a Better Manager." *Harvard Business Review*, 2022, https://hbr.org/2022/06/the-secret-to-becoming-a-better-manager

10. Gallup. "American Youth Research." *Gallup*, https://www.gallup.com/analytics/506663/american-youth-research.aspx?thank-you-contact-form=1

11. Gen Z Report 2023. Paychex. https://www.paychex.com/sites/default/files/2023-05/gen-z-report-2023.pdf

12. "Gen Z Employees Are Calling Out Workplace Bullies: What This Could Mean for HR." HR Brew. https://www.hr-brew.com/stories/2024/04/30/gen-z-employees-are-calling-out-workplace-bullies-what-this-could-mean-for-hr

13. Grady Williams, Hannah. *A Leader's Guide to Unlocking Gen Z*. Black Balsam Press, 2021.

14. Harmony HIT. "State of Gen Z Mental Health." *Harmony HIT*, https://www.harmonyhit.com/state-of-gen-z-mental-health

15. HR Acuity. "Workplace Harassment and Employee Misconduct Insights." https://www.hracuity.com/resources/research/workplace-harassment-and-employee-misconduct-insights/

16. IDEO Journal. "Turns Out Emotions Do Belong in the Workplace: Here's Why." https://www.ideo.com/journal/turns-out-emotions-do-belong-in-the-workplace-heres-why

17. Jenkins, Ryan. *The Gen Z Guide*. Ryan Jenkins, 2020, https://www.ryan-jenkins.com/wp-content/uploads/2020/02/The-Gen-Z-Guide-Final-Fully-Edited-Version.pdf

18. Knowledge@Wharton. "Managing Emotions in the Workplace: Do Positive and Negative Attitudes Drive Performance?" https://knowledge.wharton.upenn.edu/podcast/knowledge-at-wharton-podcast/managing-emotions-in-the-workplace-do-positive-and-negative-attitudes-drive-performance/

19. McKinsey & Company. "Gen Z Report." *McKinsey & Company*, 2023,

https://www.mckinsey.com/~/media/mckinsey/email/genz/2023/04/2023-04-25b.html

20. McKinsey & Company. "What Is Diversity, Equity, and Inclusion?" *McKinsey & Company*, https://www.mckinsey.com/featured-insights/mckinsey-explainers/what-is-diversity-equity-and-inclusion

21. New Yorker. "Cartoons from the August 12, 2024 Issue." https://www.newyorker.com/gallery/cartoons-from-the-august-12-2024-issue

22. Nishizaki, Santor & DellaNeve, James. *Working with Gen Z*. Amplify, 2023.

23. Paggi, Ribin & Clowes, Pat. *Managing Generation Z*. Quill Driver Books, 2021.

24. Quest Diagnostics. "Workforce Drug Test Cheating Surged in 2023, Finds Quest Diagnostics Drug Testing Index Analysis of Nearly 10 Million Drug Tests." https://newsroom.questdiagnostics.com/2024-05-15-Workforce-Drug-Test-Cheating-Surged-in-2023-Finds-Quest-Diagnostics-Drug-Testing-Index-Analysis-of-Nearly-10-Million-Drug-Tests

25. Scheiber, Noam. "Gen Z, Anxiety, and the Workforce." *Axios*, 2024, https://www.axios.com/2024/02/17/gen-z-depression-anxiety-future-workforce

26. Strauss, William & Howe, Neil. *Generations*. Harper Perennial, 1991.

27. Wall Street Journal. "Gen Z Voters Election TikTok." https://www.wsj.com/politics/elections/gen-z-voters-election-tiktok-5bcdc524

28. Woolley, Anita. "Why Diverse Teams Are Smarter." *Harvard Business Review*, 2016, https://hbr.org/2016/11/why-diverse-teams-are-smarter?utm_medium=paidsearch&utm_source=google&utm_campaign=domcontent_bussoc&utm_term=Non-Brand&tpcc=domcontent_bussoc&gad_source=1&gclid=Cj0KCQjw0MexBhD3ARIsAEI3WHIknu4uCq9skvp0BsYDlbSrF4DWf_EJq5xkvHmqYt60eqYF7dfNKxcaAjPcEALw_wcB

29. YouTube. "Workplace Emotions." https://www.youtube.com/watch?v=GON5fNGoDPk

30. YouTube. "Workplace Culture Insights." https://www.youtube.com/watch?v=DsDVCQnqcy4

www.ingramcontent.com/pod-product-compliance
Lightning Source LLC
Chambersburg PA
CBHW050317230526
45471CB00005B/2229